Applesauce on the Ceiling

Scenes from a childhood with special needs.

Rachel Unklesbay

Linda -
I hope you enjoy
the stories!
♡ Rachel Unklesbay

This book is dedicated to my brother Andrew, for providing the stories, and to our parents, for letting us live long enough to tell them.

CONTENTS

Acknowledgements

Without my mom's prompting, I don't think it would have ever occurred to me to write this book, and without my husband's consistent reminders, I'm not sure I ever would have finished it. I'd like to thank everyone who's spent time goofing off with Andrew for helping him develop his sense of humor, and those who've encouraged my parents to see the comedy in everyday life.

1 Wait—My family Isn't Normal?

In September of 1992, my mom was 8 ½ months pregnant, up on the roof helping my dad lay shingles. A passing neighbor screamed, "What are you doing up there?!"

"I'm trying to have this baby!" was my mom's reply.

She got her wish a few hours later. Mom's labor with me had been short—but my brother was nearly born in the passenger seat of the car, while the truck driver next to them glanced down nervously at my mom's feet planted against the dashboard. She was admitted to the hospital only about 20 minutes before my brother stuck his head out, opened his eyes, looked around, and then reluctantly allowed the rest of his body to follow.

The nurse on duty recognized signs of Down syndrome immediately, and wanted to get the baby away from my parents to make sure there weren't any significant health problems. My parents, oblivious, were oohing and aahing over their baby boy, thinking the characteristic signs of Downs were inherited from his parents.

"Oh, look, honey, he has your stubby little fingers!"

"And he's got bags under his eyes, just like you!"

Eventually, the nurse got Andrew away from them as he started turning blue, and the doctors diagnosed him with Down syndrome, as well as several severe heart defects. Dad, the math major, was trying to figure out the odds that the doctors had made a mistake in the diagnosis. Mom was worried about Andrew's health. Grandma and Grandpa left the hospital, unsure what to do.

I was three years old. I remember coming to the hospital, saying hello to my mom, and then climbing across her stomach to get the grapes on the shelf next to her. I don't really remember life without Andrew, though. I don't remember the first time I saw him, or held him, or anything. And I don't remember any kind of shell-shock or explanation, nobody explaining to me what a "birth defect" was. I guess somebody explained something to me, because I kind of always knew Andrew was different. But I was born with a heart murmur, so it was kind of like that, right? Right. I mean, I was totally bald until I was three. Every baby is different. Duh. It made total sense in my toddler mind, and it pretty much stayed that way as I grew up.

So when I started writing this book, I was just recording some funny family stories. As I started writing down stories, however, I realized I desperately needed organization. I wanted to know how to structure the book, and tell individual stories in a way that sounded like a real narrative.

I remembered my mom reading me snippets from *Expecting Adam*, a book by Martha Beck. My mom read it years ago, telling me some of the funnier stories from it. The book was about a woman's decision to go through with a pregnancy, despite learning that her unborn son had Down syndrome. Most of the stories my mom told me were about the author's son Adam's quirky personality. I checked out a copy from the library, thinking that if anything could help me write a book about a Down syndrome kid, it would be a book about a Down syndrome kid.

After about 100 very frustrating pages, I realized why I wasn't finding what I was looking for. I was looking for a book about a kid with special needs who does a lot of funny stuff. This book was barely about the kid at all. This book was all about the mother's expectations of perfection. The mother's pregnancy. The mother's struggles. The mother's slow realization that her son wasn't "broken."

After getting mad at the author several times for thinking any child might be "broken," and getting mad at myself a few times for putting off writing to do research in a book that wasn't getting me anywhere, it finally hit me. Before this pregnancy, Martha Beck had never had a friend with Down syndrome.

It sounds strange, but when I finally figured it out, I just kind of sat there, dazed and confused for a second. No wonder she used the word "retarded" so often. She didn't know anybody who was.

And then I thought about it a little further. What was wrong with her husband, then? Why didn't he jump in and save her—reassure her that her baby was going to be just fine, and it didn't matter if it took him a little longer to learn algebra? Oh, good heavens, I thought. He didn't know anybody either. He didn't know somebody with Downs, or autism, or anything like that. He only knew "normal" people.

But what about their neighbors? Surely someone knew! I slowly started checking off the book's "characters"—actual people in the author's life, who all expressed their deepest sympathies when they learned that her baby had a disability. None of them had a clue, I slowly realized. None of them knew someone like Martha's son Adam—at least, not personally. Not well enough to really know anything past the stigma. I couldn't make heads or tails of it. Martha Beck and her husband were both from Utah—both from Provo, where I was living. Was it the age difference? How in the world had they been stuck with all the ignorant friends, when nearly everybody I knew was totally fine with disabled people?

And, you know, you would think I would have done the math a little sooner—but I suddenly realized that, obviously, everybody who knew my family did know someone: that someone was my brother. By default, all of my friends knew a kid with Down syndrome. And for the first time, it occurred to me that my brother might be the only kid with Down syndrome they knew. *My* family was the different family.

I remembered Dad telling me about driving to and from the hospital after my brother Andrew's birth, trying to remember the probability that his son might have these specific heart defects *without* Down syndrome. I thought about him telling me that his first, absurd thought when he found out that Andrew really had Downs was that he would never be able to teach his son calculus. And I realized for the first time that my parents probably didn't know someone like Adam (or Andrew) before that, either. My parents might have been just as scared as Martha Beck. I was the only one who wasn't scared—I was three. I held my baby brother, and didn't know any different. He was a baby. He was my brother. All baby brothers were perfect, except when they had a stinky diaper.

In some ways, I do owe a lot of this book to Mrs. Beck. Her book made me realize for the first time that we all live in some kind of ignorance. Many people live in ignorance to other cultures—European, African, South American. Many people live in ignorance to the culture—I guess it's a culture—of disability. As I have recently discovered, I've been living in ignorance to the "normal" culture, where you call your siblings once in a while for advice, and they give you more than a three-word answer. Out loud.

I've never lived in another family—and since Andrew is my only sibling, I don't really have a good idea what it's like to grow up in "normal" circumstances. I'm trying to imagine what most people have been through—and this whole "normal" thing is still foreign to me.

2 THE YOUNGER (CALMER) YEARS

Andrew was an incredibly well-behaved baby. He slept all the time—except when Mom had to wake him up for feeding, he would usually sleep through the night. Everyone wanted a turn to hold baby Andrew. He was absolutely adorable, quiet, and all in all, a perfect citizen. That lasted until he became mobile.

Andrew's circulation wasn't great, and he was on oxygen constantly for the first few years of his life. He had a cannula—a plastic oxygen tube that goes to the nostrils—attached to his face at all times, usually taped there, so he would have to leave it on. This long, thin tube tethered him to an oxygen tank twice his size and about five times his weight. Essentially, my baby brother had a long leash attached to his face.

When he started crawling, Andrew would cruise through the house at top speed, hit the end of the cord, and clothesline himself by his own nostrils. He did not like the cannula.

For reasons I still don't understand, there was a hard plastic device attached halfway down the length of the cord. It was a thick, plastic cylinder, about ten inches long that ran outside the oxygen line. On each end of this cylinder, there was a thick, wavy plastic thing that looked like it was trying to imitate flower petals. As far as I'm aware, this little plastic thing existed only to be stepped on in the middle of the night, inflicting horrible pain on bare feet.

When Andrew was still crawling, he learned how to use his leverage to pull the kitchen chairs down, slamming them onto their backs. Mom was afraid he was going to pull one down on his head and be killed, so we eventually ended up with all our kitchen chairs tied upright to the table, so he couldn't move them. We ran a thin rope tightly around the table, weaving it in between the wooden chair slats as we went. This way, when Andrew tried to tip over one chair, the chairs on the other side of the table would band together, like the roots of a Redwood forest, to keep their brother chair from falling. Of course, this also meant we couldn't sit in them without untying everything first.

Twenty years later, we realized we could have just left the chairs on the floor. They would have been more accessible that way, and it's not like Andrew had the strength to put them back up after he pulled them down.

When Andrew was just a toddler—maybe even just a crawler—he had a prized, battery-operated cash register toy—a hand-me-down from me. The thing was all plastic vinyl, with numbers that punched and dinged and a button that would run the conveyor belt around and around, just like the real thing. It was a mechanized child's wonder of the early 90's.

Andrew was obsessed with this thing. He would sit in front of it for hours, just pushing that button and watching the conveyor belt. He wouldn't even put anything on it; he just watched it go around and around, hypnotized. After a while, he would get lazy and lie down, so he didn't have to go to the trouble of supporting his own weight.

One day, Mom went to check on Andrew and found him asleep on the floor. He had propped his head up against the cash register with his mouth open, pushing the button with his tooth, so he could watch the conveyor belt without having to lift a finger. Thus situated, he had put himself to sleep with the soothing drone of the battery-operated motor and the hypnotic movement of the belt.

Andrew didn't connect cause and effect very quickly—at least not behaviorally. He was fascinated with physical cause and effect; pull the chair, it comes crashing down. Wow! Look at it go! He would laugh hysterically. But indirect cause and effect eluded him. *I pulled a chair, and it came crashing down. It was awesome! Why did you make me sit in this boring corner? I want to pull chairs down again!*

Disciplining Andrew had to be done in an unconventional style. Even after the cause and effect of discipline registered, usually when Andrew did something bad, the thrill of rebellion or the spectacle of a shattered window well outweighed whatever punishment anybody could legally dole out. And typical punishments were not only ineffective, they were nigh impossible to administer. "Time out," for instance, depends very much upon the subject's willingness to sit in a chair. But when a child doesn't listen to your instructions, instructing them to sit in a chair and be bored probably isn't going to result in reform. Most of the time, it won't even result in a time-out.

Since Andrew frequently ignored the "time-out" rule, Mom and Dad had to try different tricks to discipline him. Sometimes when he was naughty, he would be sent to his room. But first, we had to take out all the toys to make sure it was actually a punishment. And when Andrew started sneaking out of his room to slink down the hall and flush bars of soap down the toilet, my parents started sending him to his room and locking the door. They felt bad, locking a special needs kid in his room, but our family firmly believes in correcting bad behavior—and it was either a forced time-out or physical violence. My parents chose the time-out over a prison sentence for child abuse.

There were other means of keeping Andrew in a time-out. One system was to take a belt or a bathrobe tie and literally tie him down, feeding the belt through the slats of a wooden chair like a seat belt. This worked for a few years, before Andrew's motor skills were good enough to unbuckle the belt—and by that time, he was willing to put himself in time-out and just sit and giggle at whatever horrible thing he had done. Clearly, time-out was not sufficient punishment.

Over time, we learned to keep him in a longer time-out by putting an egg timer in front of him so he could see exactly how long he had to sit there. This strategy doubled as incentive to behave well during time-out. If he was screaming or crawling out of the chair, all we had to do was come into the room and add five minutes to the egg timer. Suddenly, the behavioral cause-effect relationship became clear. He usually calmed down and climbed back to the chair repentant when time was added, hoping to be let off easy for "good behavior". There were a few rare occasions, however, when he ended up in time-out for nearly an hour as time kept getting tacked on to his sentence.

Once, when Andrew was about three, we were eating at Denny's, and Andrew was acting particularly obnoxious. He was yelling, spitting, and throwing things at the heads of customers. And there was no way he was going to stay in his chair. Mom was humiliated. Dad was furious. No matter what either of them did, he was still determined to destroy any chance of a pleasant dining experience for anyone in the building.

"That's it!" shouted Dad, after Andrew had done something especially bad. Dad stood up, reached for his belt and whipped it off, still visibly angry.

My father is over six feet tall, and not slight of frame. All eyes were on us, even before Dad pulled his belt off. When it looked like this poor, handicapped toddler was about to get the beating of his life, the entire restaurant stiffened.

Then Dad carefully turned Andrew's chair around, leaned down, and secured the belt around the boy's waist. "You're in time-out," he said. "Stay there." Then he stood up again and looked around.

Everyone was staring at him, most visibly relieved. Nearby, there was a gray-haired old man who was poised at the end of his chair, ready to jump in should my dad try to lash a preschooler. Dad shrugged and sighed, and the old man's muscles loosened noticeably. Then he turned around and kept eating.

3 A NOTE ABOUT WRITING

I feel like I ought to take a moment to explain something. My family is a storytelling family, and it changes the way we live, the way we talk, and the way I write these stories.

Human beings tell stories. Lots of them. It's in our nature. And while many families tell stories about their great accomplishments, mine tends to tell stories about our most spectacular failures. It's not that we don't want to move on—we just find that the stupid things we do are far more entertaining than our personal successes. "I got an A on my spelling test" doesn't make nearly as good a conversation starter as "I accidentally locked myself in my own locker today."

My family has an odd sense of humor, and we find comedy in everyday life. I frequently have to fake a cough when I realize I'm about to laugh at someone else's tragedy. When somebody falls over, we bust a gut before helping them up. If we ourselves end up in the hospital, we'll joke with the nurse. So there are times when my stories might be horrifying to someone else, and hilarious to me. If you are ever horrified while reading this book, please remember that my brother and I both survived to functional adulthood. Apparently, something went right.

In addition to a sick sense of humor, I have also inherited a family tendency to stretch the truth, which drives my husband Ethan crazy. When Ethan tells a story, he'll tell you my brother threw a piece of pizza, it hit the wall, then landed on a shelf. When I tell you the same story, I'll tell you about the perfect slow-motion arc it made through the air before it landed against the wall, sticking for a moment and then falling to leave a perfect triangular sauce stain on the paint. Ethan will get frustrated with me for exaggerating the details.

The trouble is, that's exactly how I remember it. Something in my head says, "This is about to be funny," and then everything suddenly gains

7

special effects. Things go into slow motion. I hear epic background music. And no, none of this literally happens—but this is how I often see the world, and I figure if it makes a better story that way, I should tell it that way. I'm telling a story, not an eyewitness statement.

I'm telling you this for two reasons. The first reason is that if you happen to be a just-give-me-the-facts kind of guy like my husband, this book might drive you crazy sometimes. I won't apologize, but you've now been warned. The second reason is that I'm afraid you'll think I'm exaggerating too much. I'm concerned you're going to read about a pizza-throwing incident and think, "Nobody throws pizza against the wall. She's making this stuff up. He probably just gestured, and dropped the pizza." And you can think that if you want. But know this: I never fabricate a story. I may exaggerate the details—the speed at which the slice flew, the way it hit the wall, the stain it left behind—but everyone present will tell you that the slice was thrown, and that it hit the wall. If I tell you about my dad catching my brother's pants as they flew through the air, my dad caught the pants before they hit the ground. I might get the angle of flight wrong, but the pants flew, and Dad caught them.

So call me a liar if you want to, but I'm letting you know in advance that everything in here is exactly the way I remember it.

4 Why We Can't Have Nice Things

Once he started walking, Andrew developed the disturbing trend I like to refer to as a "clearance sale". He would walk into a room, find a shelf or dresser (or any other surface with things on it), and sweep his hands along it, dumping everything onto the floor. And then he would just laugh himself silly. For months, every time I came into my room, I found all of my things in a jumbled heap on the floor. For years afterward, I learned not to keep anything on surfaces. Eventually, long after we had despaired of owning anything fragile ever again, we installed hooks on the outside of all the doors. While he was still too short to reach the hooks, at least, we could lock our rooms as we left them and protect our precious valuables from being trashed or thrown.

I liked pretty things when I was young, but I didn't have a lot of them. Part of that was because I was trying to keep up a tomboy image. A big part of that, however, was because if anything was breakable, it would be broken.

When my great-grandma died, I remember Mom taking me through her room and telling me I could choose one thing to remember her by. I was about five years old at the time. Somewhere on a shelf, I found a music box. It wasn't a typical music box—it wasn't really a box at all. It was a rotating, mirrored pedestal with two glass swans on top, and it played a beautiful song. The swans' necks formed a heart in the middle of their mirrored "pond," and I thought it was the most gorgeous thing I had ever seen.

For years, I kept this music box up high, playing it on occasion, but mostly just admiring it. I kept it well out of reach of my brother, and it survived until I was in my early teens.

That was about the time that Andrew developed a good throwing arm. I came into my room one day and found that Andrew had thrown something onto the top shelf of my bookcase, and the swans had come crashing down. The pedestal was intact, but the swans were headless and broken. I was furious, and dissolved into tears. I remember my melodramatic, teenage self crying, "I'm never allowed to have anything beautiful!" and feeling so sorry for myself. I was deep in the midst of middle school angst, and spent the evening using the broken swans as a metaphor for my shattered life. Eventually, my tears dried and I got over it.

To this day, I seldom keep fragile things. I tend to look at anything "delicate" and think, "How hard would that be to sweep off the floor?" It's not that I don't keep anything breakable; I just think of them as disposable. There are some very nice things in my home, most of them gifts from others. And if they break, I probably won't cry about it. In my early years, I learned to put my emotions in things that don't shatter easily. And in my later years, I learned that things break sometimes—but most of the time, they can be mended, and that you shouldn't live in fear of things breaking.

5 SLEEPING HABITS

Andrew always hated clothing, and he will still find any excuse to go without shirt or pants. When he was in elementary school (and later), he would come home from school, go straight to his room, and take off his clothes. We frequently found him in his room, playing in his underwear (or less).

Not surprisingly, he often tried to sleep without pajamas. Mom and Dad usually insisted he wear at least a pair of briefs and a shirt to bed, but we often came in later on to find him tucked in and stark naked. For a while, it seemed, he wanted both the freedom of nudity and the comfortable weight of cloth against his skin. He found both by stripping off his pajamas and climbing under the fitted sheet, where he would fall asleep, sucking on his fingers.

One time, Mom came into my room worried. "I need you to help me find Andrew," she said. It was well after dark. "I tucked him in, and now he's gone." We looked all over his room (including underneath the fitted sheet). No Andrew. We searched the whole house, looking in closets, beds, and in the garage. We were about to take the search outside when we decided to check his room once more. We came in silently, listening for any sound of him, and heard him breathing. I followed the sound of the breathing to one side of the room, near the toy chest. The toys, as usual, were scattered everywhere—but the lid to the toy chest was on. Gently lifting the lid, I found my brother—stark naked—asleep in his toy chest with a pillow and his favorite blanket.

6 AIR PRESSURE AND 4,000 NAPKINS

In Utah, living without some form of air conditioning can be miserable. The state is mostly desert, and in the summer, we get temperatures up around 100 degrees Fahrenheit every now and again. Usually, it stays around 80 or 90, but that's still pretty toasty.

To combat the heat, some homes have swamp coolers, which unique to dry areas. A swamp cooler doesn't suck in and cool air; it just drips water through a vent and blasts the air into the house. The result is similar to putting an enormous oscillating fan in front of a tub full of cool water.

Of course, this fan is permanently affixed to the ceiling, so you get a good whiff of air in your face every time you walk down the hallway. Growing up, I loved the swamp cooler. It spread a nice, wet smell through the house, made the air a little thicker, and most importantly, I could come in from outside and park myself right down beneath it, lying there and soaking in the cool breeze.

Another fun thing to know about swamp coolers is that, since they constantly vent air in one direction, they create a constant airflow in certain parts of the house. If we *almost* closed any door in the house, for instance, turning on the swamp cooler would suck it shut with a *slam*! "Look, Mom, the house is haunted!" The added humidity in the air would also swell the wood in the doors, so they were harder to close (or open). During the summer, we learned to throw our whole body weight into a door to open it.

Andrew somehow learned that the added air pressure would not only suck the doors shut, but also suck things under the doors. He had to find things light enough to be sucked under by air, of course. Paper was a popular choice. Eventually, he settled on disposable napkins. He would plant himself on one side of a closed door with a small stack of napkins and start placing them against the gap at the foot of the door. The thin tissue paper material would easily be sucked to the other side. When he was finished, he could open the door, collect his material, and start all over again.

Of course, this hobby was complicated by the possibility of someone throwing their body weight into a swollen door to get it open. There were a few very tearful occasions when Andrew would get a face full of door.

This activity also led to a scarcity of napkins. While Mom was glad he wasn't up to some greater mischief, she still didn't want to spend all her disposable income keeping up the paper supply. When she started rationing his napkins, he started tearing them carefully in half so they would last twice as long. Further limitations led to even smaller shreds of napkin. Soon, the entire house was covered in a tiny, white snow of shredded paper.

As an alternative to the door approach, Andrew found that he never got hit in the face by simply playing in the hallway under the swamp cooler. The vent would blow the papers around while he sat underneath, feeding napkins into the airflow. He experimented with the exact limits of the vent, discovering how far away he had to place the napkins before they would stop moving. Sometimes he just tossed them up into the air and watched them blown forcibly downward again.

One year, for his birthday, I bought Andrew an entire bulk package of disposable napkins. He opened it, grinned, and ran off down the hallway with fists full of them, throwing them ecstatically in the air like confetti when he reached the swamp cooler. All of us, including Andrew, laughed hysterically as he frolicked for hours in a hallway covered in napkins.

7 DOG FIGHTS

When I was one year old, our cousins gave us an adorable golden retriever puppy named Barney. He was a purebred, papered dog, and he grew up to be a gentle, protective watchdog. When my dad was filling out the paperwork, he just couldn't bring himself to write "Barney" as the dog's name, especially since my young cousins probably named the dog after Barney the Dinosaur. After some deliberation, the dog came to be legally known as Barnabus Winston Bisbane.

Andrew and Barney were good buds from the start. Barney would sit protectively near Andrew, keeping an open eye out for predators and pointy table corners. Andrew would hold onto Barney's back to keep his balance. Occasionally, an errant tail wag would knock Andrew onto his butt, and Barney would lick Andrew's face apologetically. When Andrew was a little bigger, he would feed Barney his toys. Barney would graciously chew a few times, then put the toys down. When Andrew was older, this friendship blossomed; we once found Barney licking the icing off a cake that Andrew had thoughtfully put on the floor for him.

On more than one occasion, Dad heard a soft whimpering sound and found Andrew holding the dog by the front jowls, sinking his teeth into Barney's nose. Barney just sat with his tail between his legs, whined, and looked up at Dad as if to say, "Please make it stop."

We had another dog later (Smedley Wallace Throckmorton) who had to go to another home because he was just too friendly. He would jump up and lick Andrew's face and knock him off of the picnic table. Frustrated, Andrew would push him off, and the process would repeat. Eventually, Andrew would resort to biting Smed's nose to get him to go away. Mom and Dad decided to split them up; I found it entertaining to tell my friends that we had to get rid of the dog because my brother was biting him.

8 Broken Glass

Andrew loved to throw his toys out the open window. We often heard giggling that seemed like it was coming from outside—in actuality, it just sounded like it was coming from outside because Andrew had his head stuck out the window to survey the mess he was creating. It got irritating having to clean up the backyard every time he ran out of toys, so Mom and Dad hot-glued the windows shut.

This taught Andrew the value of broken glass. Andrew started going through windows like most kids go through Oreo cookies. Crunched one, liked it, crunched a few more. The first time I remember Andrew breaking a window, he did it by tapping at the glass with a plastic toy power drill. We heard a crash and came running in to find him sitting buck-naked on the floor, playing in the broken glass. Not a scratch on him. Dad cut himself twice cleaning up the glass.

The next two windows to go were much the same. We replaced them faster than he broke them, fortunately, but Dad was really irritated when he had to replace the same window twice in a year. After the bedroom windows, Andrew broke the living room window at least twice—once with a Nintendo cartridge and once with his head—the master bedroom window with a plastic easel, and somehow cracked the utility room window without anybody noticing for months. Then he and I switched bedrooms and he got the one in the middle of the hallway. That window was broken several times as well.

I can remember baby-sitting Andrew while Mom and Dad were out for their anniversary, and hearing a crash from Andrew's bedroom. I came in, looking mad, and Andrew turned to face me, looking doomed. I calmed down a bit and gave him a stern lecture on the cost and physical properties of glass. He looked like he was deciding on his last meal before the executioners came home from their anniversary dinner. I decided mercy might be in order.

I came out to meet Mom and Dad as they came up the driveway. "Hi, guys. Andrew broke a window. I already cleaned up the glass and taped some cardboard over it. He's already in time-out." I was about twelve years old at the time, quickly becoming an expert in home repairs. They just sighed, then laughed. I had already punished him, so no swift retribution was at hand.

"We'll order some glass," Dad said. He was quickly becoming an expert at replacing single-pane windows.

The most impressive window Andrew ever broke was the incident with the Nintendo cartridge. He got really mad one day and just started throwing things. The Nintendo cartridge was within reach, so that was the first thing to fly. With reckless abandon, he flung it sideways, and it cut straight through the glass like butter. The pane didn't shatter. There was just a circular hole in the middle of the window, like Catwoman used to do in the Batman cartoons I had watched behind Mom's back. I opened my mouth to yell at my brother, and just kind of left my jaw open there for a minute. "You're still in trouble," I told him. Then I went over to admire his work.

One time, our neighbor was out for a jog and rang our doorbell. "I can hear Andrew laughing evilly," she said. (She actually used the word, "evilly.") Our backyard gate was usually padlocked—not against intruders, but to keep Andrew from wandering off, into the street or into the next-door neighbor's house. Someone had left the gate unlocked, and Andrew had come into the side-yard between our house and our next-door neighbors'.

Our neighbors were a sweet couple in their 70s or 80s, who always remembered our birthdays and never quite understood why Andrew sometimes snuck into their garage to open and close the garage door. I think they saw Andrew as a rather tall toddler; once when Andrew had been sneaking into their garage, Bernice set up baby gates on either side of their car to keep Andrew from getting through. She had even put pillows under the car to keep him from going under. Andrew, at least six years old at the time, had simply taken down the baby gate.

This particular day, however, Andrew snuck out of the backyard and found a pile of huge limestone rocks in our driveway, leftover from a recent home improvement project. When we found him, he was busy throwing slabs of rock over and over onto the hood of the neighbors' car. This was where our jogging neighbor found him. The windshield was cracked in several places, and the whole hood was dented. Mom was both furious and ashamed. Her son was vandalizing the elderly.

The total damages were around seven hundred dollars, all of which were covered by the insurance. Since my marriage, my husband has tried to teach me to barter for a good price, but I'm convinced my mom has accidentally stumbled upon the ultimate haggling weapon: tears. Through worried sobs, Mom told the insurance agent about her suffering finances and her medical bills for her handicapped son who needed heart surgery only weeks after birth and who still kept breaking everything in sight no matter how she tried to teach him or punish him and (gasp) she should just be grateful that he was still alive but she had no idea how she was going to pay for any of this (gasp) and he would probably just do the same thing to someone else's car next week. The insurance agent proved to be an excellent counselor, gently reassuring my mother that everything would be alright, and quickly approving the entire cost of the repairs.

(My mom says this account is exaggerated. She's probably right; I don't remember the conversation. I was a kid, and my mom talking with an insurance agent wasn't worth eavesdropping on. All I know is, Mom was crying at some point in the conversation, and all of the costs ended up covered.)

9 HOW I BECAME A REPAIRMAN

Andrew liked to watch his favorite videos again and again and again. Most kids go through a *Dumbo* phase, or a *Jungle Book* phase, or (in my case) a *Scamper the Penguin* phase. Andrew moved from phase to phase as he destroyed tapes or our parents hid them.

This was back in the day of VHS tapes, so Andrew could watch the video, then watch the video rewind, then watch it going forward again. The cycle would loop, forward and backward, until Mom told him he could only watch it once more. Then he would wait until she left the room, rewind ten minutes, and hit "play" again. Next time Mom left the room again, he would rewind. After a few hours, Mom would finally catch on and take the tape away from him.

Later on, Andrew sped up the process by fast-forwarding to all his favorite parts, then rewinding and watching the highlights over and over. Mom confiscated *The Princess Bride*, because she was disturbed when Andrew became obsessed with the torture scene.

We kept a steady supply of spare VCRs in the garage. Mom and Dad got the idea one day, shopping for a replacement after Andrew had broken one. Instead of buying one replacement, they bought two: then when the first one broke, they could replace it the same day and go buy another spare to keep in the garage.

I got pretty good at basic VCR repair. We never replaced a machine we couldn't fix ourselves—which meant there was a long time when the cover of the VCR was left unscrewed, so we could just lift it off and see what was going on inside. Sometimes it was just worn out, or a gadget was out of place. And sometimes we found a peanut butter sandwich inside. Or a fork. Or a puddle of vomit. At times like these, the machine was usually beyond repair.

As Andrew grew older, he never outgrew the tendency to obsess over things, whether they be his favorite movies, his favorite children's books, or his favorite music. Eventually, sometime in his teens, we figured out that he was autistic as well as having Downs. The autism, as far as I'm aware, may have contributed to his need for structure and predictability. Perhaps it's the reason he can listen to the same song on repeat for upwards of seven hours; he knows what's coming.

Regardless of whether autism is to blame, there are certain films and artists I will never be able to tolerate again. Some of his favorite CDs have been burned into my brain deep enough to make me flinch when I hear a few notes.

The more surprising part is that there are some movies I'll still watch with him. *The Nightmare Before Christmas* is still one of my favorites, even though I can quote every line and probably describe the stage directions of every character. And we watched so many Wile E. Coyote cartoons that I sometimes get the background scores stuck in my head.

10 STARTING SCHOOL

When we moved from Salt Lake City to Bountiful, I was about to enter fourth grade, and Andrew was about to start Kindergarten. Mom called the elementary school, wondering if they could refer her to a good school for kids with special needs. They surprised her by telling her they had a thriving Special Education program, and Andrew would be welcome to come to Bountiful Elementary. More than that, the Special Ed. program was completely mainstreamed—meaning that Andrew would spend the whole day in a class with all the other "normal" students, with an aide occasionally pulling him into the hallway to do math or spelling on his own.

Mom was in tears. Up until that point, she had never thought anyone would place her son on the same level as the other kids his age. She was floored to think he would be in the same classroom as everybody else—even after she had warned the school administration about his behavioral problems.

As it turned out, our new neighborhood was a step up for me and a flat-out miracle for Andrew. Bountiful Elementary had the best Special Education program in the state, and parents sent their kids from all over. The mainstream program ensured that every student in Special Ed. had friends their age from all over the academic spectrum. More than that, after a few years, my mom volunteered to set up a "buddy" program; each classroom assigned weekly "buddies" to assist the special needs student in their classroom. This meant that every week, Andrew had assigned friends shepherding him around, reminding him not to throw things, and playing with him at recess. At the end of each week, Andrew and his helpers got to go to a party with all the other buddies in the school.

The program helped Andrew with his behaviors and social skills, but more than that, it built an entire community of understanding and tolerance. Every student who went to that elementary school had at least one friend with special needs. Many of these friendships continued into junior high and even high school. As a result, my community—and my generation specifically— was incredibly aware of special needs.

Possibly as a result of this, I never heard the word "retarded" used as an insult until I got to college. I was aware the word existed, because my dad once explained the meaning of the word to me and told me why it was offensive. Aside from that, I don't remember hearing the word at all until I was nineteen. I was completely floored when I came to a church school and started hearing people dropping the slur commonly. (This was especially strange in a Utah community where most of the students used swear words such as "freak," "fetch," "crap," and "flip.") I asked a friend why he used the word, and he said it was no big deal. Sure, it was rude, but no ruder than calling someone stupid. I disagreed. To me, calling someone retarded because he was acting stupid was just as insulting as calling someone gay or Black or Mormon because he was acting stupid. It insulted the wrong party. To me, it sounded something like, "Wow, Scott, you're just as dumb as Rachel's family!"

After the first few shocks, I started to realize I was going to have to deal with this on a fairly regular basis. I started coming up with ways to point out that the phrase was insulting without going on a tirade. It's often difficult to get your point across briefly, but when you get it right, it can be just as effective. Probably the most direct approach was to simply look up after someone used the word and say quietly, "I have a brother with Down syndrome. Please don't use that word."

My dad came up with a more humorous approach. Once, when his coworker had done something she regretted, she apologized to someone else and called herself "retarded." Dad interrupted the conversation, pointing to the offending woman. "My son is retarded," he said. "What you just did was stupid. You don't have an excuse." Fortunately, the woman found the comment funny and apologized again—this time for using a word she hadn't realized was offensive.

After a few years of this, I had to reevaluate the way I handled the word. For a summer, I worked with autistic adults in a day program. One of my coworkers was complaining one day about her boyfriend, and referred to his behavior as "retarded." I flinched, but then realized that none of the other people in the van—all of whom were technically, medically, retarded—seemed to mind. Some probably didn't notice, but those involved in the conversation shrugged it off, realizing that this woman would never have used that word to describe them. She didn't see them as retarded. I didn't correct her, because I realized I was the least qualified person in that van to take offense. If the rest of the van was okay with it, I could get over it.

I'm not saying I think we should all use slurs. I still don't use the word myself. But when it's clear a person isn't trying to offend, it just doesn't sound offensive to me anymore. I've had to think through the way I react; if I assume my brother should take offense, does that mean I'm assuming he *is* retarded?

Well, medically, he is. But if the definition of the word has started to change, and the word just means someone's acting stupid, then maybe it doesn't fit anymore. Certainly, if someone spat the word at him, they'd get a right hook in the face. But I think I'd react the same way if they spat any other word that meant "stupid." Because he's not, and that's my brother you're talking about.

I don't think the word ought to be common. Because it's an insult, and those shouldn't be common. But as far as political correctness goes, I don't think I can really hold myself up as a shining beacon; I make fun of Andrew all the time. Usually when he does something weird. Because he's my brother, and he knows better. He knows he's supposed to wear pants in public, for instance, and not my mother's underwear. That's a thing I'll gladly tease him about. Personally, I draw the line between embarrassing and humiliating. If it's funny, and he'll laugh too, I'll tell the story. If he's going to feel bad when I tell it, I shut up.

11 Forks, Spoons, and General Hysterics

Table manners don't exactly run in our family.

My dad will gladly bring up subjects that should not be discussed at the dinner table, including genocide, politics, and bodily functions. My brother and I have been known to blow straw wrappers at each other's faces in public. (We learned the trick from our grandpa.) My mom is arguably the most civilized person in the household.

While Andrew was a toddler, he developed a hearty love for some of his favorite foods. He nearly died at least a dozen times when he insisted on eating half a banana in one bite. He quickly learned the signs for "toast" and "peanut butter." Green vegetables were a different story. In fact, anything that wasn't toast, bananas, or applesauce was likely to be rejected.

Andrew would spend hours at the dinner table, refusing to eat what was on his plate. Mom didn't expect her kids to clean their plates at every meal, but she did expect us to try everything, and she often told us we could be excused from the table after a certain number of bites. Andrew would take about twenty minutes to psyche himself out for each bite.

He also tried bartering, which sometimes got him a reduced sentence. Eight bites is better than twelve. But when those eight bites take forty minutes to get down, it's still a rather hopeless view.

He took to sneaking away from the dinner table. Unfortunately for Andrew, his idea of sneaking worked about as well as a lead balloon. He would sulk in his chair, then suddenly his face would brighten. He would look around to make sure nobody was paying attention. (This was fairly conspicuous, although I'm sure he thought we never noticed.) Then he would slowly start sinking in his chair.

His sulk would bring him lower and lower, until he slid like a snake off of his chair and onto the floor under the table. He would then begin shuffling on his hands and knees, very slowly (and loudly) making his way toward his room.

Of course we noticed. It's hard to miss a ten-year-old crawling over your feet and occasionally giggling at his own genius. And we'd usually wait until he was out in the open before Mom or Dad would call out, "Andrew, come back to the table."

Andrew would freeze. And when it was clear we could still see him, he giggled again and waited until we stopped talking to him. Then he started shuffling again, slowly.

"Andrew."

He froze again, sometimes dropping flat to the ground. If he didn't move, he seemed to think we couldn't see him.

"Andrew, you're not invisible. Come eat your green beans."

This usually continued until someone physically picked him up and transported him back to his chair, where he sat looking devastated.

One year, Andrew developed a running gag. Every day, when we sat down to dinner, Andrew dutifully sat (cross-legged) on his chair. We all bowed our heads and closed our eyes to pray. As soon as the prayer began, Andrew grabbed his silverware, pulled his T-shirt out in front of him, and dropped the silverware down his shirt to bounce off his chest and clatter onto the chair beneath him. He laughed.

And laughed. And laughed! He would laugh until tears were coming out of his eyes and his breath came in desperate gasps. He would laugh until he was drooling. We would pause the prayer and compose ourselves, trying not to show any reaction that would encourage him (which is difficult to do, when the kid next to you is beside himself, hysterical). After a few long minutes, he would get himself under control, and the prayer would continue.

And then he would do it again. Grab the silverware, drop it down his shirt! Clang! Hysterical laughter! It was so funny sometimes he fell out of his chair. On a good day, it only took us two tries to finish a hurried prayer and start eating.

My reflexes became strangely honed. After a few weeks, I could catch his hand on the way to the silverware—sometimes with my eyes still closed. That was funny, but not nearly as funny as if he got away with it. One time I beat him to it and dumped the silverware down my own shirt. That just made him mad, though. It was his joke, not mine. Besides that, Mom and Dad were annoyed with me for encouraging him.

For some reason, it was no longer as funny after the prayer was over. Once we said, "Amen," our risks of clattering silverware went way down. And for some reason, it never even occurred to us to pray before setting out the silverware.

12 Flying Food

For a solid decade, our kitchen ceiling was never clean. The first few times pudding hit the ceiling, Dad cleaned it off. After a while, though, it became difficult to motivate him to clean a spot on the ceiling that was only going to be splashed with applesauce two hours later. A textured ceiling only added to the difficulty. Over the years, Andrew honed a specific muscle set that allowed him to flick his leftovers deftly upward about six feet in the air.

On one occasion, this skill set sent a full pitcher of orange juice flying across the room. It splashed across the wall art above the piano in a beautiful, tropical cascade of color. The carpet was stained forevermore. (We later learned to buy brownish, splotchy-colored carpet, so the stains wouldn't stand out.) The piano, fortunately, was cleaned off easily. The picture on the wall was framed, but the glass had been shattered by some earlier airborne hazard; now it was hanging on the wall unprotected, and the photo took the brunt of the damage. I believe that picture had to be replaced, but for a few months, it hung there with a lovely orange tint to one of the corners and a bubbly, water-damaged texture.

There were, of course, other foods that were fun to throw. Fried eggs were one of Andrew's favorite breakfasts—but in typical picky-kid fashion, he insisted on sunny-side up, lightly steamed so the yolks had a thin skin over them, salted, peppered, and runny enough to dip his toast in. The toast also had to be cut into squares, folded butter-side in. When his toast was gone, the eggs no longer held any purpose, and he threw the leftover egg whites wherever he felt like the room needed some country décor. Mom saw this as a waste of her food and cooking efforts, and insisted that Andrew eat at least most of the egg white. She started to cut the egg up into manageable pieces for him every morning when his toast was gone. He responded by gesturing wildly at his plate, rocking his head back and forth, moaning dramatically, and expressing general displeasure at the idea. After a few minutes, he would (almost tearfully) resign himself to taking a few bites. Then, once Mom left the room, tiny egg pieces would litter the kitchen.

Tomato soup was (and still is) a common stain to find on the walls. Andrew would never throw a whole bowl of soup, but by flicking the spoon, he could send a few drops into oblivion, and we would never find them in time to clean them up. Dried tomato splatter-paint would slowly accumulate on the wall next to the egg stains. He still sometimes splashes the last few drops of his milk or juice onto the wall, just for kicks and giggles.

The walls are still speckled, although I occasionally make a few bucks by cleaning them while I'm home for a visit. Last Thanksgiving, my husband Ethan and I asked for a chore, and ended up scrubbing a considerable amount of egg yolk and apple juice off of the kitchen walls. It took us about half an hour, but we were pleased with the result: the walls were one solid color again, and they looked a lot better.

13 VACATION

No childhood account would be complete without a few vacation stories. Any family who's ever packed their kids into the car for a few days of relaxation has learned, through long and painful experience, that the most relaxing part of a vacation is coming back home again. Unless, of course, you get a babysitter and go without the kids—and my brother was ill-behaved enough by the time he was walking that my parents were reluctant to leave him with anyone less skilled than a lion tamer. As such, our parents went without a break from us for about two decades.

In our house, preparation has always been the most time-consuming part of a vacation. My mother and I are polar opposites when it comes to packing. I take after my dad: pack a swimsuit, a toothbrush, and an extra pair of underwear. If you're going to be gone a full week, pack a change of clothes and a book. If your clothes get dirty, you can always wash them in the sink.

Of course, this leads to problems, and even my dad teases me about having to go to Wal-Mart on vacation because I forgot to pack contact solution, a warm jacket, socks…something. But I can't help but think, "I'm on vacation—I deserve a new jacket, anyways!"

My mom, on the other hand, wants to be "home away from home." And that includes all the things she normally uses at home. Toothbrush. Shampoo. Lotions. Outfits. Mustard. Whatever she might need, she packs. She wants options, and she wants all the options she would normally have.

Leaving the house, therefore, has always been the most difficult part of any vacation. I can remember years when we were going to leave at 6am, and ended up leaving around 10. Mom spent hours painstakingly putting what seemed to be the entire medicine chest into large plastic bags, just in case one of the bottles exploded in the car. Dad and I would sit on the couch, dozing, and Mom would get increasingly irritated that we weren't helping her pack. We would respond that we had packed everything the family could possibly need, and it was already in the car.

Andrew's health needs only fed this flame. We now had to bring every medication he normally took, every medication he might possibly need, a basic first-aid kit in case he picked his scabs in the car, and an oxygen tank and cannula cord, just in case his circulation was poor and he started turning blue. Add to that the difficulty of keeping the kid amused, and we began packing electronics, toys, videos to play once we reached our destination—anything we thought would keep him entertained. The stuff would accumulate in the trunk, between and below the car seats, and sometimes in the laps of the passengers. There were only two kids in my family, but we never had leg-room on road trips—and half the time, we had enough stuff piled between us that Andrew and I could barely see one another.

This, of course, was a good thing. I've heard stories about "normal" family dynamics on road trips, and it seems like ours were fairly similar. Most family trips, I understand, include such games as "Slug Bug" (or "Punch Buggy"), "Find the Alphabet," and "Stop Touching Me." In our family, we had a similar dynamic, but usually without words. I read a book in the backseat until Andrew got bored. Once that happened, my chances of peace and happiness dwindled considerably, and we began games of "Stop Touching My Shoulder," "Leave the Stuff on Your Side," and "Mom, He's Trying to Tickle My Eyeball!"

The introduction of the GameBoy in later years helped considerably; then we could ignore each other in peace for upwards of 5 or 6 hours while we played Pokémon or Super Mario Bros. Of course, this only lasted as long as the batteries.

Surprisingly, most of our vacations went without a hitch. I have many fond memories of beaches in Oregon, horseback riding in Yellowstone, and hiking through Zion's National Park, and none of these memories include any serious destruction from (or of) myself or my brother.

Of course, when I was younger, I probably wouldn't have noticed if something had gone wrong unless it had gone sensationally wrong. But given our family track record, you would think this would happen every time we left the house.

There are a few vacation incidents I do remember. One year when Andrew was still a baby, he got locked in the car while we stopped by a roadside fruit stand in Oregon. All I really remember is Mom crying and Dad being very ornery while he picked the lock with a coat hanger. I was off somewhere nearby, obliviously eating fresh blackberries or plums.

Years later, Dad took us on a day trip to Pavont Butte, a unique land plateau in the middle of the Utah desert. I'm sure the place is quite scenic to those who haven't seen a desert before, especially if you go in the spring or fall. This particular day, however, it was over 100 degrees outside, the only suitable picnic spot we could find was in the middle of a little-used gravel road, safe from the prickly sagebrush, and Andrew, who was questionably potty-trained at the time, filled two big-kid-sized Pull-Ups with poo one right after another. After Dad changed and cleaned up Andrew (the second time), we started climbing the butte, which required clambering up a 45-degree angle of loose dirt and rock. There was no shade. Dad carried Andrew over his shoulders. Halfway up, he turned around to see Mom red-faced and panting. "I hate you," she told him for the first and only time since they were married. Dad turned around, and we went home without ever reaching the top.

The official "Vacation from Hell" happened when Andrew and I were teenagers. We went camping in Zion's over the summer—again, on a week that reached 100 degrees. That is, it was 100 degrees in Salt Lake—on the north side of the state. We were camping on the south side of the state, near the Arizona border, where it was about 10 degrees hotter. We had also passed up the campground near the river, because Mom was afraid Andrew would fall in and drown. (Dad still claims the vacation would have been fabulous if Mom had relented on this point. I think it would have needed to be 20 degrees cooler before anyone sane would have gone camping.)

While my parents unpacked, I amused myself by drawing in the dust with a stick; the desert was too hot for most plants, and the campsite was mostly rocks and dry, cracked earth. While I drew in the dirt, Andrew drew on the car with a rock. When Mom and Dad discovered this, they were less than pleased. They put him in "time-out" in the tent by keeping the zippers closed with a safety pin. This is where he discovered a squirt bottle of sunscreen and gave the tent interior a fresh coat of white, 35 spf paint.

Later in the week, we went hiking to Emerald Pools—which was cool and beautiful—but Andrew was too tired to make the return trip, and Dad had to carry him the whole way down. Aside from the hike, the only entertainment Andrew found that week was escaping to the outhouse, where he could blow on the flies that gathered there and let them land on his arm, tickling him. Delightful.

After several days of begging, Mom finally got Dad to concede to packing up and coming home early. Dad got a speeding ticket on the way home, and asked to pose with the policeman. We have the picture as a souvenir, documenting our worst-ever camping trip.

The Camping Trip from Hell was the only vacation I think we ever disliked, but that didn't make vacations uneventful. Most of the quirks, however, were not Andrew's doing. Our tire blew out on the side of the road once, and we found a repair shop in Nebraska operated by a toothless old man and a guy with a peg-leg. One year, our transmission went out on exactly the same stretch of road where I had totaled my first car a few weeks before—and with the same song on the radio. (I no longer listen to Fastball's "The Way" while driving.) And of course, any time we happen to be headed south, there's a cheese factory my father simply can't drive past. Regardless of whether we've decided to stop for cheese curds, he always finds a way to "stretch his legs" at that particular exit.

Shortly after we were married, Ethan and I drove my family down to southern Utah on a three- or four-day vacation. While we teased Mom about how much stuff she had brought, Dad told us he had kept Mom from packing the toaster. She has Celiac disease and can't eat anything that's touched gluten (including gluten-free toast from a contaminated toaster), and she was just concerned she wouldn't be able to eat anything at the hotel's continental breakfast. She laughed as we mocked her, saying she had realized packing the toaster would be a little ridiculous. Meanwhile, Dad muttered, "Well, you did bring the blender."

"Wait—you brought the blender?" I whirled around in the front seat, hoping Dad was kidding, but she only confirmed that she had brought not only the blender, but at least two pounds of raw spinach leaves.

She leaned forward, excited. "We're going to make smoothies!"

14 CREATIVE SIGNING

By the time Andrew was in fourth grade, most of the kids at school knew him. All the kids in his grade either liked him, or pretended to like him because the teacher expected them to be nice to him. And he was a pretty funny guy, which meant he was fairly popular.

But because he didn't speak very often, he used sign language. Most of the kids in the fourth grade knew a few signs: hurry, bathroom, play. There were a lot of kids at our elementary school who had speech problems, and while American Sign Language (ASL) wasn't taught as a language class, most of the kids ended up with at least a basic playground vocabulary.

We ran into problems sometimes when Andrew would invent his own signs. None of our family was fluent in ASL, so if we didn't know how to say something, he would just come up with his own way. Andrew invented a sign for "garage door," for example, that we later discovered to mean "cheese." It took us a while to find a new sign for "door," and even longer for us to convince him that the old sign was going to get him a cheese sandwich, not a chance to push the button for the garage door. Every time we tried to get the point across, he just looked at us like, "You know what I mean. Why do you care how I say it?"

Andrew's favorite school lunch, served every Thursday, was mashed potatoes and gravy—but the best part of the meal was the dinner roll that came with it. Andrew was obsessed with those rolls. There were days when we would use rolls as a reward for good behavior—"if you're really good at school, we'll go to the bakery and get a roll!" Oh, wow. Best motivation ever.

Andrew had his own sign for "roll." We had a sign for "bread," but we could never find anything more specific than that, so we just shrugged our shoulders and used his sign. Soon, the entire fourth grade was well familiar with the new vocabulary word, and used it all day on Thursday, getting Andrew pumped up for his favorite meal. Everybody was excited about lunch—and now everybody was excited that Andrew got a roll!

Unfortunately, Andrew's sign didn't mean "roll." After the whole school had been using the sign for several months, a new school aide—who spoke a little more sign than we did—quietly informed us that the sign Andrew was using actually meant "vagina." Now we had to set about the task of teaching the entire fourth grade a safer sign and eradicating the old sign. This was made more complicated by the fourth grade sense of humor: if we told the kids the old sign was a bad word, they would only use it more often.

Eventually, we found a sign for "biscuit" and settled on that. We started using "biscuit"—and only "biscuit"—as our sign for "roll." We refused to acknowledge the old sign from Andrew, insisting he change. And we slowly started correcting the fourth graders, in small groups, explaining, "the old sign was just one that Andrew made up. This is the real sign." It took another few months to make the change, but to this day, Andrew uses the sign for "biscuits." And I don't think any of his classmates ever figured out why we made the sudden change.

15 HIDDEN TREASURE IN THE HEAT VENTS

At home, Andrew became obsessed with heat vents. A heat vent could provide hours of entertainment, because anything you put into the slats would disappear with a clatter and never be seen again. We gradually began to lose all our silverware. Then our CDs. Old newspaper clippings. Pens. Erasers. Photographs. Medical bills. Refrigerator magnets. One time, my parents sent me hunting around in the heat vents (I had the smallest arms), and I came up with about 30 spoons, some knives and forks, CDs, crayons, plastic toys, an obituary, some magnets, and a picture of Jesus.

I got stuck in that heat vent for about half an hour, with my arm wedged tight. It wasn't a very pleasant experience. Eventually, I wiggled my way out, while Mom and Dad tried to give helpful tips. My arm was swollen and scratched for the next day or so.

Dad eventually cracked the system by getting some fine wire mesh and installing it just behind all the vents. This way, the hot air could still come through, but nothing was small enough to go through the mesh. For the first few weeks after installing the mesh, Dad would find CDs or other small objects wedged into the slats of the vents, or hovering just behind the slats, stuck in the wire. But it was fairly easy to dig things out when you could see them that clearly, and after a while, Andrew realized that it just wasn't as much fun anymore. He left the heat vents alone.

16 A Few Words About Poo

For every baby, there comes a day when a diaper simply is not enough to contain everything. Most of the time, diapers work on a sophisticated, clockwork system. The baby goes so many hours (or minutes, depending on age and digestive constitution), the diaper gets bulky, the diaper is changed, and the baby is happy and dry for the next so many hours.

Some babies, however, are ticking time bombs, ready to leave mess, stench, and carnage in their wake.

My brother was a time-bomb baby. My brother was also a time-bomb toddler. And then he was a small time-bomb child. Until age nine, he simply never found sufficient motivation to reserve his bodily functions for the toilet. And in nine years, a human body can produce an awful lot of poo.

The diaper situation in our household was a two-edged sword. The first downside was the simple magnitude of the problem: a Pull-Up worn by a nine-year-old is physically a much bigger mess than a diaper worn by a newborn. On Bring Your Child to Work Day one year, Andrew decided he had had enough, and soiled himself sensationally. Dad took him into the office bathroom, stripped him down, washed *all* of his clothes in the sink, and threw away his socks.

The second part of the problem was Andrew's artistic streak. When Andrew was still rather young—three or four, perhaps—my grandparents came to babysit one evening while Mom and Dad went out on a date. Upon returning, Mom found her parents sitting on the sofa in the living room, with shocked, vacant expressions on their faces, staring straight forward. They were barely responsive. While Mom questioned them, trying to discover the fiendish thing we had done to them, Dad came to find me and Andrew. He found us both in Andrew's room: I had put Andrew in

34

time-out, and was busily wiping down the walls, which were covered in feces the same way most children would cover the walls in finger-paint. I was about six or seven.

I have no doubt that Grandma and Grandpa did everything a normal baby-sitter would need to do. I just think they were expecting to watch some young, rambunctious kids—not a tiny artist who specialized in bodily materials and his overly pragmatic sister.

When Andrew was closer to eight or nine, we had a jungle gym in his bedroom for a while. It was one of those plastic play-sets you put in the backyard: it had four interlocking walls with some ladder steps cut out of them, and a slide on one side. This was one of the only toys Andrew was allowed to have, because it was too big and heavy for him to break a window with.

This play-set made Andrew one of the coolest kids on the block. A play-set in the backyard is fairly normal, but a slide in your bedroom is way beyond awesome. When you position the bed at the base of the slide, you have achieved a maximum-fun zone. My friends and I used to beg to hang out with Andrew, so we could turn off the lights and play on the play-set, holding glow-in-the-dark stars in our hands so we could see where everybody was. It was like watching a whole gang of falling stars playing tag. Andrew tolerated us, but after a while, he would get sick of the dark and blind us all by turning on the light without warning.

This was our favorite game until Andrew discovered a new way to play with the jungle gym. We came into his room one day, investigating a horrible smell. Although his Pull-Up was relatively clean, we could tell there was poop somewhere. ("Find the Poop" is probably every parent's least favorite game.) When we searched his room, we discovered a smear of poo all the way down the slide: the kid had pulled down his pants, sat at the top of the slide, then pooed his way slowly down until he reached the bottom. He had then wiped his butt neatly on the plush carpet at the base, pulled his pants back up, and left his room to play somewhere more aromatic.

This incident removed any sympathy for his "inability" to potty train. Whenever people told Mom that he "didn't know any better," she just raised an eyebrow at them.

Although the play-set was plastic, and easily sanitized, this incident also removed any desire my friends and I had to play on it. The jungle gym was quickly relocated to the backyard, and Andrew's status as the cool kid took a pretty solid blow.

Later on, when I was in college, I remember sitting at a restaurant with a few of my friends. They were exchanging "accident" stories; a few had peed themselves in dire circumstances, a few had more serious problems. (Most of the "more serious" variety were told about "a friend of mine.") A lot of the stories took place in Brazil or other far-off places, while getting accustomed to a new diet or a newly found parasite.

While patrons near our table were probably turning a little green, my friends and I were laughing, and I was much quieter than usual. Finally, one of my friends put up his hands and protested, "You guys, we'd better stop. I think we're grossing Rachel out."

I snapped my head up, surprised. I realized I had been quiet for a while, lost in thought. "I don't think you understand," I told him. "I'm not quiet because I'm disturbed; I'm just trying to figure out which stories I can actually tell in present company without somebody losing their lunch."

My friends appeared intrigued, so I explained something of my brother's artistic ability. They wanted a specific example of a story that might disgust them, so I told them about the time I came into my brother's room and discovered that Andrew had found a way to cover more ground by throwing fecal matter onto the ceiling fan and letting the contraption spread the mess for him.

There was a pause, and then someone asked, "You mean to tell me that it actually hit the fan?"

"Well, yes," I laughed. "I suppose it did." That was the only story I told that day, but I don't think it was ever beaten.

Shortly after discovering the ceiling fan trick, Andrew found that a ceiling fan could do lots of other things as well. For instance, if you throw a wet Pull-Up onto a ceiling fan and turn it on, eventually the centrifugal force either sling-shots the wet diaper across the room or rips it apart, showering a beautiful cascade of urine-soaked crystals across the room. Picture an enormous litter box, all of it fragile enough to crush when stepped on—or run over with a vacuum. Few things are as frustrating as slowly scooping crystals off of the floor, knowing that one wrong move will leave a urine-soaked patch behind you. My mom is not easily angered, but she was known to mutter to herself while cleaning up these messes. Dad, on the other hand, usually escaped this variety of clean-up, as Andrew's prime inspiration usually came during normal working hours.

17 The Disappearance of a Nerf Ball

When Andrew was about 10 or 11, he had a very strict limit on the kinds of toys he could keep in his room. Because of the frequency of broken windows, he wasn't allowed to keep anything hard or heavy, unless it was too heavy for him to lift. As a consequence of this, his only furniture was a bed and a bedside table. All of his "dangerous" toys were kept under lock and key—almost literally. His closet door had a hook-and-eye at the top, securing it shut for all too short to reach.

Usually, Andrew was allowed to have one toy "checked out" at a time. This meant he could keep his marble-works out, but if he wanted to play with something else, he had to clean up. He was usually okay with this, but it made Mom feel bad to look into his room and see that ocean of bare carpet. She felt like she was keeping her son in a prison cell or something.

So, in came the squishy toys! The room looked much less deserted with a few stuffed animals and Nerf balls lying around. Some of them Andrew liked; some he just ignored. But he always had a few toys he could play with, and Mom had a little more peace of mind. I think this was about the same time I bought Andrew a Nerf ball and over-the-door basketball hoop. I would come into his room and we would just sit on his bed, shooting hoops.

Andrew's room was a fairly organized chaos. To him, it was organized. To us, it was chaos. Chaos and stuffed animals. When one of his toys went missing, nobody noticed for days. Every now and then, the room had to be cleaned (usually after the ceiling fan had scattered a Pull-Up everywhere) and we would find toys Andrew had completely forgotten about.

One day, Mom brought a Nerf ball out of his room to show me. It had a huge bite taken out of it. I want to clarify here: There wasn't a huge "chunk" ripped out of the Nerf ball. It was a bite. There were teeth-marks.

The dog never came on the carpet. None of my friends would have bitten a foam ball. I certainly didn't do it. Andrew's friends seldom came over, and certainly wouldn't have bitten his toys. And Mom, worried that Andrew might have actually eaten the chunk, searched high and low in that bedroom. She tore the place apart, but never found the missing chunk. He had eaten a Nerf ball.

Our suspicions were confirmed a few days later, when Mom was helping Andrew in the bathroom. He was sitting on the toilet, obviously constipated, when it occurred to Mom that the Nerf ball might be to blame. Upon further inspection, she found it was indeed the Nerf ball. Mom had to use chopsticks to get the foam chunk out—and no, we never ate with those chopsticks again.

18 ANDREW'S NEMESIS: GREEN VEGETABLES

In my family, there are not picky eaters. As a child, there were certain foods I didn't like. Mushrooms, for instance. Green peppers. Onions. Olives. Pickles. You could say I was a pretty picky eater, or at least I would have liked to be. But that didn't exempt me from eating any of the above. If Mom cooked it, you at least had to try it. And you thanked the cook profusely.

Andrew, however, seldom fell into the category of those who thanked the cook profusely. When peanut butter sandwiches or canned ravioli were served, he was overwhelmingly grateful. Most other foods brought about melodramatic arm movements and tragic facial expressions. This demonstration was especially dramatic when green foods were served.

It didn't really matter what the vegetable was; if it was green, it was offensive. We began to notice this pattern one day when Mom asked, "What's wrong?" to Andrew, who was looking mournfully at his plate.

Looking up, he signed, "Green," and his open lips pursed into a square as though he were about to throw up. This tradition continued for months afterward, every time green food appeared.

The best tantrum my brother ever threw over vegetables was the day he created a sign for asparagus. Mom dished out the food one plate at a time, and when she put several asparagus spears on Andrew's plate, his face froze in horror. He stood there for a minute, staring at it, then shook his head violently and started moaning.

"Andrew, what's wrong?" Mom asked innocently, knowing full well she had just placed green on his plate.

Andrew screwed up his face, focused all the energy in his body, and released it with a violent, repeated motion. His hands flew away from his mouth and toward the plate over and over again, as he made loud vomit noises. For about five seconds straight, he pretended to throw up all over his asparagus, then looked up accusingly at Mom, lower lip trembling.

We were laughing too hard to help him deal with the trauma the asparagus had caused. Fortunately, he lightened up when he saw us laughing, and eventually ended up eating at least a few bites of asparagus. He wouldn't admit it, of course, but he seemed to like them.

19 Oh, the Things You Can Burn!

The oven was a source of endless amusement for Andrew. Most kids become fascinated with the oven when they realize that's where cookies come from. An oven is a magical place where lumpy dough goes in and poof! Delicious things come out. How is it done?

Andrew didn't really care about cookies. He became fascinated with the oven when he realized that most household items are flammable. I learned a quick lesson in fire safety when I was about ten years old and he put a bathrobe tie in the oven when nobody was looking. Mom turned on the oven to preheat, and soon smoke had filled the kitchen. When we opened the oven to find out what had happened, we found a smoking rope coiled on the bottom, one end gently flickering. Mom dragged the tie out onto the floor and beat it while, under her direction, I poured baking soda all over it to smother the flame. Andrew stood in the hallway, enthralled. He was a little concerned when the flames left the oven—but once the fire was out, he was all smiles. What a show!

His "open flame" stage was mercifully short, and moved quickly toward the "acrid smoke" fascination. He quickly discovered the chemical properties of plastic, and started putting twist-ties, milk carton caps, and empty water bottles into the oven. The resulting smell was horrible—and our reaction was apparently well worth it. After a few months, he discovered that if you put a full water bottle in the oven, it would smoke *and* steam. On one occasion, he put a full bottle of baby oil in the oven, and nearly set the entire kitchen on fire.

He never turned the oven on, fortunately. He just set the trap and let someone else turn it on. We soon learned to check inside the oven for bits of plastic before attempting to cook anything.

20 ANDREW'S FIRST SENTENCE

Andrew found a certain joy in throwing milk on the windows. He would ask for a glass of milk, drink half of it, wait until you weren't watching, and then, splat! White liquid hit the window and dripped slowly down the glass.

Once my mom heard Andrew pouring himself a glass of milk. He drank half of it, and Mom came into the room to make sure he wasn't going to splash it. He saw her and froze, poised halfway between his seat and the window, glass in hand. He couldn't have looked guiltier. The two of them just stood there for a minute, waiting.

"Mom. Go. Please," said Andrew, loudly.

Mom was stunned. This was the first full sentence Andrew had ever said on his own.

"Okay," she said, so pleased to hear him speaking that she willingly followed his instructions. She went.

Splash!

And then she came back and made him clean the window.

21 HORROR AT THE DOCTOR'S OFFICE

Most children have an innate fear of the doctor, and Andrew was no exception. The fear usually stems from the first time they go for shots. They toddle into a doctor's office naively one day, and come out having endured traumatic stabbing with only a few Band-aids and some stickers to show for it. Some kids recover quickly, some don't.

Andrew didn't. I can't say I blame him, either. While most kids go to the pediatrician once a year for a check-up—maybe facing a shot or a scary tool for looking inside the ear, Andrew had regular appointments for his heart, his ears, and just about everything that ever went wrong. Because he was born with multiple heart defects, Andrew had heart surgery when he was still only weeks old, and regular cardiology appointments after that. The doctors seemed to want blood work every time he blinked.

Andrew's first pediatrician was a doomsday prophet. Perhaps he was just covering his bases to prevent malpractice lawsuits, but his diagnosis was usually a vague hint at Andrew's imminent demise. My mother was a basket-case for the first few years of Andrew's life, as Dr. Doom kept telling her not to expect her son to live much longer. After Andrew surpassed his first few dozen "expiration dates," however, Mom started gaining confidence, stopped asking how long he had to live, and switched doctors.

Andrew, of course, was not told any of this. As a growing toddler, all he knew was that the doctor's office or hospital meant he had to endure the horrors of drawing blood. For a small child, a needle-stick is frightening enough without having to leave the needle in and watch your own bodily fluids come out through it. And Andrew was not the most cooperative small child.

He developed a rare fighting technique at a young age. He employed a combination of thrashing with reckless abandon, going limp when least convenient for the adults nearby, and then biting. My dad was taking martial arts lessons for most of Andrew's childhood. The martial arts instruction began as physical therapy for an injury, but it came in handy at the doctor's office. Dad sat down, pulled Andrew onto his lap, and crossed his legs around Andrew's to keep them still. Then he crossed Andrew's arm across his chest and held it there, while two nurses held out the arm they needed to stick with a needle. During all of this, Andrew convulsed and frothed as though he had rabies, and threw his head back in hopes of connecting with Dad's chin.

This behavior became the routine at the blood lab, and continued well into Andrew's teens, until one day it seems Andrew resigned himself to his fate and decided to be a "big boy" about it. As Dad prepared for battle one day in the blood lab, Andrew sighed, sat down, and held out his arm. Dad was stunned. Andrew still pouted and pointed out his bandaged arm for the next few days, but it seems the fighting was over.

Of course, that didn't mean the fear was. Andrew was late to potty-train, but even long after he figured out the whole toilet thing, Mom learned to take him to the bathroom as soon as they entered the clinic. And then again, ten minutes later. And probably just before they left, just to be safe. Even with these precautions, Andrew usually lost it as he entered the clinic, his own personal torture chamber. He learned to face his fear with a stiff upper lip, but his bladder and bowels remained unconvinced.

He now has better control of his own body while at the doctor's office, and will even take comfort in the usual routine he finds there. He'll help the doctor check his heart with a stethoscope, then point out the instruments for looking down his throat and into his ears. He'll insist on checking his blood pressure, and giggle as the cuff inflates. But he still gets very squeamish around needles, especially at the hospital. He's had several hospital visits that included an IV, and he does not like the idea. At the doctor's, he'll point to the back of his hand (where the IV is usually administered) and look visibly distraught, looking for reassurance that he won't be given an IV.

This concern extends to others as well. Anyone he's ever seen in a hospital gets a thorough check-up whenever Andrew sees them again. When he visits our grandpa at home, he'll point to Grandpa's chest, where he's seen stitches from a heart surgery. Then he'll check Grandpa's hands for needles. After making sure Grandpa's alright, he can carry on with normal life. We have several neighbors who always get this check, as well. After a few months or years, he'll eventually move on and leave the memory in the past—but until that time, he has to make sure his family and friends have recovered sufficiently from their hospital visit.

22 TROUBLE IN SCHOOL

Given his behavior at home, it was surprising that my brother was only suspended a few times during elementary school. Although his behaviors in school were more than enough to get a "normal" kid suspended, his Special Ed. teachers realized that when a kid acts out because he's bored at school, sending him home will only come as a reward.

The only times I can remember him being suspended, it was when he threw scissors (or a stapler—I don't remember which one), and when he pushed a girl down the stairs. He was stuck behind her, and she was taking too long descending because she was on crutches.

When Andrew was suspended, Mom went well out of her way to make sure it was a miserable experience. He was not to leave the house, play with toys, or eat anything pleasant. His social activity was restricted to me, Mom, and Dad—all of whom took every available opportunity to remind him that he was grounded because he had pushed a girl on crutches down the stairs, and that wasn't nice, and it probably hurt her, and it made her sad. It might even make her go to the doctor (a horrifying thought). You get the gist. By the time he got back to school, there was no guarantee he wouldn't act up again—but it was usually a week or so before he was willing to push his boundaries (or his classmates). Being bored is the worst punishment in the world.

The closest I've ever come to an all-out brawl happened when I was in 6th grade. Andrew was in 3rd, and we went to the same elementary school. I was walking past Andrew in the hallway between classes when I saw him make a beeline for the vending machines. A girl had just bought a soda, and Andrew grabbed her change before she could take it from the machine, "running" ("shuffling" is closer to the truth) to escape with his booty.

"Big-sister mode" engaged, and I realized I had only a split second to act before my brother learned to steal other kids' lunch money. I also knew that, because he had special needs, nobody was going to blame him for stealing the money; he was going to get away with it. And he knew it. He was working the system. My 8-year-old brother was becoming a criminal.

So I tackled him. I was bigger than him, so I didn't have to bring him to the ground to incapacitate him. I had him in a Half-Nelson while I tried to pry the coins from his stubby fingers. He howled. I calmly explained, "This money isn't yours. You have to give it back." He howled again and threw his head backwards into my chin.

I not-so-calmly repeated the order that he give the money back. He went limp and flopped his body every which way. I went limp right along with him and held on tight. I wasn't willing to hit him, but I can't say I was altogether gentle at this point, either. I was determined to get the money out of his hand.

By this point, the girl by the vending machines was looking extremely awkward. She was hesitating between walking away, standing by to gawk, and breaking up the fight. "It's okay," she told me. "Really, it's just a couple cents. He can have it."

I raised my head to glare at the girl. "*This is not about you!*" I hissed as Andrew clawed at my chest. She didn't appear comforted, and settled uneasily against the wall to watch the fight play out.

We wrestled for what seemed like hours (and was probably seconds). There was biting, scratching, kicking, flailing, and screaming. Blood was drawn. Feelings were hurt. Nipples were twisted. And the teachers walking down the hallway, unsure whether to side with or against the special needs child, just slowed down and gave us a wide berth as they walked on by.

Eventually, I emerged with the small change, handed it to the girl (who ran off quickly with it), and told Andrew he wasn't allowed to steal. Battered and sniffling, we walked our separate ways—he to his classroom, and me to the nurse's office.

23 GUARDIAN ANGELS

At the church service when Andrew was blessed, Dad felt inspired to bless him that he would have guardian angels going before and behind him, keeping him safe.

Andrew has abused this privilege. When he was about two, he pulled a heavy drawer out of a filing cabinet, and it sailed over his head to slam to the ground behind him. As a child, he would frequently put his hand on the hot stove to see whether it was on. Unburned, he would stare at his hand, perplexed. It would be a little pink, at most.

Dad frequently cut himself cleaning up the broken glass after Andrew had broken a window. Andrew would be untouched.

Andrew loved dogs, and frequently made friends with strange pit bulls by walking up to them and shoving his hand down their throats. The owners would yank back on the leash, horrified. The dogs, unfazed, would cough a little and spit out the hand, then lick out the inside of Andrew's mouth.

Andrew had a very mechanical mind, and loved to see how things worked. He was especially fascinated with the lawnmower. One day, while Dad was mowing the lawn, he saw Andrew suddenly running toward him. He had a long stick in his hand, determined to shove it into the blade and see what happened. Dad released the handle, which killed the motor, but the blades were still whirling when Andrew shoved his arm under the mower. Dad moved to block him, but the blade had chopped up the stick and struck Andrew's hand three times before Dad pulled him out of harm's way.

Miraculously, Andrew's fingers were all still attached. In fact, he hadn't even broken any bones or severed any tendons, let alone lost any fingers. The doctors were amazed. He didn't even need stitches; they just gave him some bandages and antibiotics, as a precaution for whatever germy horrors lived on the mower blade.

The biggest challenge of the lawnmower incident was keeping a bandage on the kid's hand. At the time, Andrew was around ten—quite old enough to get any bandage off in only seconds. But in order to keep his hand from getting infected, the doctors said to keep it wrapped up until the skin closed. Dad bandaged the hand. Andrew ripped it off. Dad re-bandaged the hand. Andrew tore it off again. Dad taped the bandages. Andrew took the tape off with his teeth.

In order to keep the hand bandaged, it ended up swathed in bandage after bandage after bandage, all underneath a sock, which was duct-taped to some extra bandaging on his arm—the only way to keep the sock on. Although only a few fingers were cut, Andrew ended up carrying the equivalent of a cotton baseball bat wrapped around his arm.

The first day he showed up to school with bandages, we were running late. I had to drop off Andrew at the elementary school before Mom could drive me up to the junior high. When I showed up with Andrew, his teacher stared at the horrifying bandages all over his arm. "What happened?!" she gasped.

"Lawnmower." I said. And then I left. When Mom picked him up that afternoon, his teachers swarmed her with questions. Was he okay? Should he be in school? Did he still have a hand?

Mom pampered him for a day or two, feeling sorry for his injury. When he used his "bat" to break the glass in front of the church fire extinguisher that weekend, however, sympathy went out the window. One more window broken, and with an injured hand. No injury from the broken glass, of course. But he did give the lawnmower some distance for the next few years.

24 Soap and Water

Did you know you can melt a whole bar of soap out of a toilet U-bend?

It's really easy. You just boil a big pot of water and pour it into the toilet while flushing—about fifteen times in a row. It melts the soap, so it doesn't clog the toilet. And so nothing else sticks to the soap and clogs the toilet.

Of course, this whole process goes faster with a drain snake.

And it only takes a few hours!

25 LEARNING TO PEE AGAIN

Potty-training can be a difficult or boring transition for kids. I think it's fairly common for children to "hold it in" when they need to use the restroom. For young children, the toilet may be frightening. For older children, the toilet is an inconvenience, interrupting valuable time spent with Legos or a GameBoy. I'm not sure what Andrew's problem was—maybe he just found his time in the bathroom boring—but for a few solid months in his early teens, he refused to pee until absolutely necessary.

Over time, his bladder control became impressive, and he started going hours on end without using the toilet. This was a good sign for his potty-training skills, but it became alarming when we discovered there were times when he was actually going all day without relieving himself. The sense of alarm escalated when Mom (who usually supervised bathroom visits to prevent soap bars from being flushed down the toilet) discovered that Andrew was going days without peeing. More than that, he was clearly having trouble urinating. A small stream was the best he could do most days.

I don't remember whether a doctor was consulted, but Mom and Dad made the decision to set aside designated bathroom times, trying to get Andrew's body back on schedule. They also pumped him full of fluids, hoping to flush out whatever was blocked. For about a week, Andrew still didn't pee. More than that, when we insisted he drink something, he usually just threw it up.

By this time, Andrew was in significant pain, and it looked like he was smuggling a football in his abdomen. While he seldom communicated anything verbally, his face showed he was not having a good time of it. We knew his bladder was way bigger than it should have been, but we didn't know much else. We decided to take him to the doctor.

I think I had school that day, so I wasn't with him during the doctor's appointment. Mom and Dad tell me, however, that this was the only time they *hoped* the trip to the doctor's office would scare Andrew into wetting his pants. Sadly, it didn't, and he spent his time rocking back and forth in pain instead. A nurse came in, asking all kinds of questions—most of which were unanswerable, because Andrew wouldn't tell anyone specifically where he hurt, and what the pain felt like. Mom and Dad told her something was wrong, he couldn't pee, and he probably needed a catheter to drain his bladder. His kidneys were likely backed up, which was why he was in so much pain. The nurse calmly went through some more paperwork, ignoring my brother's moaning. She eventually looked down at Andrew, who was on all fours on the floor, screaming.

"What is he doing?" she asked my parents quizzically. She seemed to think this was typical behavior for a child with special needs. (To her credit, I'll admit that for some children, this *is* typical behavior.)

My mom gave the nurse a funny look. "He's screaming," she said. "He's in pain."

"Oh!" The nurse looked visibly surprised, then went through the rest of the paperwork much more quickly. When the doctor came in, he told my parents that Andrew could come in for a catheter in a few days, when they'd have an anesthesiologist available.

"No," said Dad, "this happens today. Either you can do this here, or we'll take him to Emergency. It's up to you."

After some hemming and hawing, it was decided that Andrew was probably in enough pain that any relief would be welcome, even without anesthesia. He got a catheter, and his bladder started draining into a bag.

After filling one bag with urine, Andrew's mood improved considerably. He stopped screaming, and even gave a few relieved laughs as he watched the bag fill. After the second bag filled, the doctors saw fit to send him home with the catheter still in place, and it stayed there for a few weeks. The doctor's opinion was that Andrew had spent so long training his body not to urinate that his muscles refused to release. He spent so long trying not to pee, his body forgot how.

Everyone felt bad that Andrew had been in pain so long, so he got pampered for a while. He got all his favorite foods, and finally held down his favorite drinks. We had a few embarrassing moments when he wanted to pull down his pants and show everyone what the doctor had done to him. This continued for months after the catheter was removed, as he wanted to "talk" about his horrible ordeal. Fortunately, his body seemed to figure things out, and he never needed the catheter again. And in time, he even stopped bragging about the experience, much to my parents' relief.

26 IT'S A SMALL WORLD AFTER ALL

When I was about fourteen, Mom and Dad took us out to eat at Winger's one day and said they had a surprise for us. They handed us a bunch of those raffle tickets you can buy in rolls of billions, and told us to solve the puzzle. On the blank side of the tickets, they had written letters. I started trying to spell out a sentence. After about fifteen minutes, Mom finally took mercy on me and told me it was all one word.

All one word? This word must be huge. Mom was getting impatient, excited to see my reaction when I got it. I, on the other hand, was completely without a clue. What in the world? With a good deal of prompting and hints from Mom, I ended up spelling out: D-I-S-N-E-L-Y-A-N-D.

Disnelyand? What in the world is a disnelyand? Mom was freaking out, waiting for me to realize something. Andrew was eating a quesadilla, ignoring us. Dad was laughing his head off. And I was still confused.

"Dis-nel-yand?" I sounded it out. Surely that couldn't be it. It sounded Yiddish to me. Possibly Greek. I could tell by their hysterical laughter that Mom and Dad thought I was getting close. Maybe it was Latin. Was this the name of a dinosaur?

After about two minutes of puzzlement, I finally said, "Disneyland?"

"*Yes!*" shouted Mom. Dad was laughing too hard to speak. The waitress was probably rolling her eyes at all of us.

I was still confused. What about Disneyland? It took me another few seconds before it dawned on me that *we* might actually be going to Disneyland.

I had some misgivings about the trip. I acted excited, but honestly felt like this was going to be a weird vacation. Mom had been using the phrase "Disneyland" to represent unlimited and unattainable happiness for years, the same way I might use the phrase "bacon-wrapped ice cream." I faked enthusiasm for her sake; she looked like she had just won the lottery. But I secretly thought it was going to be lame.

Mom was the only one of us who had ever been to Disneyland before, and it was when she was about five years old. So the only thing she really remembered was "It's a Small World." And her description of it didn't sound quite as "magical" to me as she seemed to remember it.

"You go from room to room, and there are all these puppets in costumes from around the world, and they sing, 'It's a Small World.'" I had something in my head comparable to the little wooden puppet show in *Shrek*. Gee, Mom. Sounds great.

So when we actually rode the train around the park, I realized how much bigger this place was than I'd imagined. And when we went through Small World, I was simply blown away. Dad and I were seated at the front of the boat, and when we turned to look at Mom and Andrew, they were sitting side by side, both weeping openly—Mom because she was reliving her childhood, and Andrew because he was just moved to tears.

I have no idea why Andrew was so moved by that ride, but he became obsessed with it. The entire week we were at Disneyland, he insisted on riding Small World at least three times a day. And every time, he cried. He was so excited about it, we searched every gift shop until we found a CD with the ride's actual theme music. After we came home, Andrew would listen to that CD in his room and cry all over again.

Andrew had a distinct advantage at Disneyland: he had special needs. Not only that, but he had obvious, visible special needs. People gave us their place in line. When he got tired out, Mom and Dad got concerned about his heart condition, and we rented a wheelchair. This got us to the front of the line for most of the old rides, since the wheelchair wouldn't fit in the queue. We rode Pirates of the Caribbean about four times in a row before the pirate at the handicapped entrance guilted us into finding another ride.

When we got to the Indiana Jones ride, I already knew what to expect. I was blown away by the quality of the ride, of course (being used to Lagoon, Utah's big attraction), but my friends had told me all about the huge boulder that just *almost* smashes you at the end of the ride.

Andrew, however, had heard none of these stories. Nor had he seen any Indiana Jones movies, to the best of my recollection. He was just excited to go on a cool roller coaster. This one had statues with glowing eyes and explorer stuff everywhere, and it bumped and jerked all over the place! How exciting! At the first few bumps, he was laughing at the thrill of riding, and fascinated with the atmosphere around us. There were cool things everywhere!

As we drove through the Ancient Ruin of Special Effects, we

nearly fell through a rickety bridge, stared into the eyes of a forbidden idol, and encountered horrible creepy-crawlies. As we rounded a corner and saw holographic tarantulas skittering across one wall, Andrew shrank away from the wall and looked at me, disgusted.

"They're not real spiders," I said "They're pretend." He laughed carelessly, as though he had known it all along—but he looked a little relieved.

He spent most of the ride laughing or poking my shoulder and teasing me when I shrieked as the ride bucked or something jumped out at us. But toward the end of the ride, he suddenly saw a boulder the size of a small house coming toward us.

He pointed at the boulder, tugging my arm. "I know," I said. "It's okay."

He looked at me like I had just told him that the Brazilian cockroach was a variety of camel. He pointed more adamantly, with a look that said, "No, seriously—you must not have seen it."

I repeated, "It's okay; it won't hit us."

At this point, his face clearly showed that he was despairing of my ability for intelligent thought. He looked wildly around him, looking for the turn, thinking we must surely be turning away from the boulder. Something had to save us. It wasn't there; we were going straight for the boulder, and it was coming straight toward us. There was nothing for it.

At this point, it looked like Andrew was considering abandoning ship. If there had been enough room—and enough time—he might have actually gotten out of the car. But I think he knew he didn't have enough time, or perhaps he was preoccupied trying to save his idiot sister, who refused to see reality even when it was eight feet in diameter, staring her in the face. I, meanwhile, was glad the lap bar made it difficult for Andrew to bail out.

As the boulder came toward us, he squeezed his eyes shut and ducked, grabbing my arm and just waiting for the end. The track then took a quick drop downward, ducking neatly under the boulder, which rolled on behind us and off the side of the track somewhere. I tapped his shoulders, and he risked a glance up. He looked around. No boulder. Glanced behind us and saw the boulder, just above and behind us, and added up what had happened. He started laughing—nervously at first, then louder as sheer relief kicked in. Within ten seconds, the laughter had turned to bravado. He guffawed, looking at me the same way he had after the holographic spiders. It was a look that said, "Ha! I knew it all along. Boy, you sure were scared."

It still took him a day or two before he would go on the ride again, though.

27 ECONOMICS 101

After Andrew's first visit to Disneyland, he wanted desperately to go back. He would sign, "Disneyland," then grin. I would explain to him that we couldn't go to Disneyland today: we didn't have enough money. He would sigh and look troubled, then sign, "Tomorrow" hopefully. No again. "Next week?" Nope.

This went on for weeks, and he was nearly in tears some days about it. Since he was fairly good at math, (and I was tired of having this conversation,) I decided to teach him a few things about money. I took a large empty can from our food storage supplies, cut a hole in the plastic lid, and asked Andrew to help me put Disney stickers on it. Then I got out some spare change, and put it into the can. "See this can?" I asked. "When we have a thousand dollars in this can, then we can go back to Disneyland."

His eyes lit up immediately. He ran to raid Mom's purse, and I had to stop him. "You have to earn the money," I said. "You work, I'll pay you to work, and you put the money in here, okay?"

He was off like a flash! In record timing, he had made my bed, vacuumed the floor, cleaned up his toys, and taken out the garbage—all for pennies. (I later felt bad for cheating him, and raised my rates.)

As soon as Mom came home from the store, Andrew went flying into the kitchen to talk to her. He signed: Mom. I. Want. Money.

"Rachel! What did you do?!" Mom yelled at me. I felt perfectly justified. I had taught him a valuable lesson about math, society, and Disneyland. Furthermore, the entire house was spotless.

I didn't have to do my chores for a week. Eventually, he started asking for higher prices than the quarters I'd been paying him. After realizing just how much a thousand dollars was, he started asking ten dollars to make the bed. I refused, telling him I would give him fifty cents. He would wander off, scowling. Later, he would ask a dollar. I didn't budge.

After a bit of haggling, I would just ask him, "Do you want to make the bed, or am I going to do it?" He would finally make the bed for the fifty cents, realizing that it was going to be made either way—he might as well get the money.

The Disneyland bank actually did get us to Disneyland again. Ordinarily, Mom and Dad would have waited until they had a really good income tax return (which is what made the first trip possible, I believe) or until Dad got a raise before even considering going back. But seeing Andrew work harder than any of us to earn money was impressive—and made the rest of us feel a little guilty. We started sneaking our spare change, or even dollars, into the bank when he wasn't looking.

Obviously, a thousand dollars wasn't going to fit in a bank the size of a coffee can. Mom developed a system of counting out the change in the can and emptying it every time there was twenty dollars in it. She put the money in the bank (not to be touched, under any circumstances), and then she let Andrew put a sticker on a chart, marking twenty dollars closer to Disneyland. That way, he knew we were still keeping track of the money—and he had a visual graph of how close he was to his goal.

It took about two years to save up the money, but with incentives for some extra daily chores, Andrew was making at least a dollar a day. We ended up needing over a thousand dollars, but with all of us saving, Mom and Dad decided they could cover the extra cost. In fact, they booked the trip before Andrew had actually filled up his chart. We wanted him to feel like he had really earned the trip, though, so we still wanted to get all those stickers filled up. During the two weeks before we left, Mom suddenly became a human ATM, offering twenty-dollar bills to Andrew for whatever chores she could think up. Inflation skyrocketed in our home for a month—but Andrew earned his way back to Disneyland.

28 HUMAN GPS

I believe that most people are a genius in at least one area. For some, it might be math or science or music. Others have excellent communication skills. Some are fantastic at puzzle games. My mother has an uncanny ability to remember information about diet and nutrition. My father and I are both excellent at mapping out a city in our heads.

My brother's genius far surpasses ours, however. My dad and I can give you directions to just about anywhere in the thirty miles surrounding our home. My brother can navigate you anywhere he's ever been in his life.

My parents first noticed this talent when Andrew was a toddler. He was signed up for "Kindermusic" classes at a studio about thirty minutes from home. Every time Mom drove him there, he got excited to see his friends and dance to the music. Every time Mom drove anywhere else, Andrew would start bawling as soon as we passed the freeway exit to his Kindermusic class. A few times, he slept through the drive, woke up on the freeway far past the exit, and started crying. He knew we'd passed his favorite destination.

This gift became more apparent as he grew older. There were long road trips when Andrew would suddenly start freaking out for no apparent reason. Clueless, we would try to calm him down any way we could, only discovering an hour later that Dad had taken a wrong turn. Andrew's mapping ability became most apparent as we drove from the airport to Disneyland the second time. Andrew pointed to every turn we needed to take along the way, giggling as he came closer to his beloved Small World. He navigated us successfully from the airport through the highways of Los Angeles until we reached the same hotel we'd stayed in during the past trip. He had only been on these roads once, when we had driven to California—two years before.

I took Andrew out for dinner one day when I was in high school, just for the fun of it. We went to the Olive Garden, where he flirted with the waitresses (and got all the breadsticks he wanted), and I took a wrong turn on the way back. We were about half an hour from home, and I was wandering aimlessly through the residential streets on the side of the mountain. Finally, I stopped the car and looked at Andrew. "Which way is home?" I asked.

He hesitated, not sure what to do with his newfound power. After a few more prompts, he pointed right. I turned right. "You're in charge," I told him. Every intersection, I asked him which way to go. He pointed, and I obeyed. The experiment proved two things: Andrew not only knew exactly where we were and how to get home, he also knew exactly where every railroad crossing was along the way. It took us well over thirty minutes to get home, but he enjoyed every minute of it.

29 Trainspotting

There's a lot of daily wonder that we just skip over. Take your average John Doe and stick him in a car. Now put a slow-moving train in front of him, and make him wait while the train passes. Chances are, he'll turn the car around if he can. If traffic has pinned him, he'll slump down in the driver's seat, curse silently to himself, and tap the steering wheel impatiently, knowing that this distraction will make him at least five minutes later to that important thing he was about to go do. If he's particularly solutions-oriented, he might start coming up with blueprints in his head for a new, elevated train system, so that nobody would ever have to stop for a train again. Better yet, an underground system—so nobody would have to hear the rumble or see the engines go by.

But for Andrew, trains were the main attraction. Trains were the reason you got in the car in the first place.

When Andrew got stopped by a train, he stopped dead in his tracks. He stopped for the same reason a man stops to look at a beautiful woman. He stopped for the same reason a child stops in front of a balloon vendor. He stopped for the same reason safari explorers stop for a grazing rhinoceros. He begged us to turn the car around when the train was *behind* us, so that he could sit right up close to it, roll down the windows to hear the thundering, and rock back and forth in the backseat, moved to tears by the beauty and power of the thing. He laughed and cried every time, no matter how many times he'd seen it before, because every time, he was still impressed.

Sometimes I can't help but wonder why we all push this man so hard to be more "normal."

30 ANDREW DABBLES IN WRITING

For a while, Andrew got excited about writing.

Now, when I use "excited" here, I don't mean "excited" like he was excited over Disneyland. More like he was "slightly inclined to consider writing as an option." But compared to his "excitement" about speaking out loud, he was ecstatic about the idea. The point is, he was willing to write when that was the best way to get his message across—and any form of communication was better than none at all.

Andrew wrote notes and lists, frequently adding his favorite foods to the shopping list Mom already had on the fridge. He occasionally wrote short, disjointed love notes to the cute girls at school. The best uses of writing by far, however, always happened in church.

My brother and I used to make connect-the-dots games on the church programs during especially boring meetings. (We seldom got in trouble for this: my parents are the ones who taught us how to do it.) When Andrew was writing, however, we took to carrying around a yellow legal pad, and we would pass notes back and forth silently.

To the casual observer, these notes might be a little non-sequitor:

"What do you want to do when we get home?"

"Vacuum 10000"

This meant he wanted to vacuum the house. The 10,000 referred to his expected payment, in dollars, for fulfillment of this chore.

"$10,000? That's too much! I can't pay you that much!"

He would giggle, then start adding zeroes to the end of the number.

"Vacuum 100000000 Disneyland"

"In your dreams, man."

Now and again, new words would crop up in the exchange, and I had to figure out what they meant through trial and error.

"Home ravioli goat"

"You want to go home and eat ravioli… with a goat?"

"Yes home ravioli"

"What about the goat?"

"Mom"

"Is Mom going to eat a goat?"

"No"

"What about the goat?"

"Mom"

"Is Mom a goat?"

"Yes"

I handed the page across to Mom, who read it and burst out in a fit of barely contained whispering. "I am not a goat! Why did you teach him that?" I told her I didn't teach him anything about goats. While Mom was accusing Dad, Andrew took the pad back, laughed, and wrote:

"Mom goat"

This was his favorite punch line for the next several weeks.

31 JEEVES

Sometime in his teens, we discovered Andrew wasn't acting typical, even for a kid with Down syndrome. For years, we'd assumed this was just because he was a weird kid in a weird family. But after a while, we started taking him to see behavioral therapists.

Turned out, Andrew was also autistic. This explained a lot of behavior, like his strict need for order and a schedule. He wasn't the only one in the family with compulsive tendencies, but his were definitely the strongest. Mom and Dad actually got a lot of significant clues about Andrew's behavior once they started looking up more information about autism. We started keeping a cleaner house, for instance; that meant more order in Andrew's environment, and therefore, Andrew's brain. He stopped crashing things around as often.

Of course, that didn't mean he stopped leaving a mark wherever he went. There came a period when Andrew and I were both a little obsessive-compulsive. I had my room immaculate, with the chair facing the bed, a green blanket draped over the chair just so, a laptop case (and laptop) in the far corner, and a soft armrest on the bed. I would leave for a few minutes, and Andrew would come in, throw the armrest and blanket behind the bed, move the laptop to the corner behind the door, and sit on my bed. I would come in, move the laptop back, and pick up the blanket and armrest to put them where they belonged. It got to a point where neither of us even realized what we were doing. You could always tell who had been in my room most recently, based on the arrangement of the room.

I still like my room just so, but I've loosened up a bit. In Andrew, however, this has led to a behavior known in our home as "Jeeving." "Jeeving" was so named because Andrew reminds us of a butler ("Jeeves"), walking slowly through the house, finding things out of place, and quietly putting them back where they belong.

The trouble is, Andrew's idea of "where they belong" sometimes differs from ours. Frozen hamburger, for instance, "belongs" under the worktable in the kitchen. Toilet paper, along with all canned clams, "belong" in the kitchen garbage. Unopened soda cans "belong" in the dryer. Compounding this difficulty is the ever-changing arrangement of "belonging." One week, Mom's prescriptions "belong" in her purse. The next week, all pills in the house must be flushed. Today, my car keys might go in my room; tomorrow, the top shelf in the refrigerator.

To this day, visitors to my parents' house (including myself) are encouraged to lock their belongings in my old room—the guest room—for the duration of their stay. Anything placed on an open surface is subject to confiscation, and may never be returned.

32 URBAN LEGENDS

As Andrew and I got older, I started to notice people's reactions to him more and more. I started wondering whether the odd looks we got in fast food restaurants were because we were using ASL, or just because he looked a little different. And once we started going to different schools—middle school for him, high school for me—I started noticing the way people reacted when I told them my brother had special needs.

There was always a tendency to forget to mention it. It wasn't the first thing on my mind. Plus, it was entertaining to say something about my brother waltzing into the front room with no pants on, and then telling my friends that he was fourteen years old.

One phenomenon I still notice when I tell people my brother has Down syndrome is the way people immediately begin talking about it, whether or not it's relevant to the story. A few people will ask what that is, or how it affects him. Some people will share stories about someone they know who has Downs, then ask if Andrew does anything like that. I'm totally okay with these two reactions; they seem to be pretty standard conversation to me. What's weird is when someone says, "Oh, yeah, I know a kid with Downs... he's a pretty cool kid." And then leave it at that. I feel like it's the special-needs equivalent of saying, "My best friend is Black." That's nice and all... but it's irrelevant. I just remind myself that people need a way to connect, and if they don't know very many people with special needs, they're grasping at straws to relate to anything I'm saying.

What's really weird is when another Mormon shares a story (an urban legend, given how often I've heard it) about a friend-of-a-friend-of-a-friend whose kid once received a spectacular blessing. This friend will tell me or my parents all about how this Downs kid was told he was such a valiant spirit in the war in heaven, before coming to Earth, and how Satan vowed to get revenge on him any way he could. God gave him Downs so

64

he wouldn't be fully accountable for his actions, and Satan couldn't tempt him the way he could tempt others. The storytelling usually concludes with the logical fallacy, "So Andrew was probably one of those who personally escorted Satan out of heaven when he rebelled!"

Wow, I think. That was pretty elaborate. Tell me more about my brother.

These stories usually come from those at least a generation older than me—a generation less comfortable with special needs—which leads me to believe the person is trying to "console" my parents, reassuring them that there's nothing really wrong with their son. Some of them seem to think they're just sharing a really cool doctrine they learned that only applies to my brother and people just like him.

But that's just it—there isn't anyone just like him. If I had a blessing that told me why I had brown hair and never quite grew as tall as I had wanted, that would be great. But that would apply to me. Just me. If somebody has a spiritual experience that tells them why they have Down syndrome, I think that's a beautiful, personal revelation. But that only applies to them. And frankly, I'm not really sure how they'd feel about people spreading the tale far and wide every time they see somebody with Downs.

For all we know, Andrew was given Down syndrome because he stuck his fingers in the Celestial Light Sockets one too many times, and God decided he needed shorter fingers to keep out of trouble. I don't know.

My brother is an individual. He has some tendencies common to Downs kids. He has some tendencies common to autistic kids. He has some tendencies common to Copes, and a few common to Keeners, and quite a few that are spectacularly all his own. So when new parents ask me how they can help their special needs child, I usually tell them it depends entirely on the child. Each child is different.

33 Sock Wars

One year when I was in high school, Mom bought us all socks for Christmas. And when my mom does something, she goes all out. When Mom buys you something as boring as socks, she wants to make it exciting. So she buys you an entire bucket full of socks, rolled up in little fluffy white mounds, and puts the words "Snowball Fight!" on the bucket.

How adorable, Mom thought.

How foolish, we thought.

Within hours, Andrew and I were flinging socks at each other with gusto, ducking and weaving behind the tables and in and out of doors. Neither of us had very good aim—but you know, that wasn't really the point, anyway.

This continued off and on for the next few months. Every now and again, Dad would be lying on his bed, reading, when I would come running in, bound over the bed (and my father), and scream, "Hide me, save me, hide me, save me!" I would hide behind the bed as Andrew came running down the hall, laughing wickedly, wielding a pair of socks in each hand. Sometimes he didn't find me immediately, and I would have a few seconds to sneak out and reload. And sometimes, he found me and pelted me relentlessly. But then—

"You're out of socks, little man!"

Panicked running down the hallway again.

34 I Get Hit in the Face

When Andrew loses his temper, things can get ugly. Usually, things also get airborne. Once, when I was arguing over something with Andrew, he lashed out and threw the remote control.

Andrew has a good arm—but not very good aim. This is good, provided he's actually aiming at you. If he's not, however, you might be subject to friendly fire. On this occasion, Andrew was aiming at the window, and hit my nose. I was standing about three feet in front of him, so the remote smashed into my face pretty hard.

My first thought was, "Punch him in the face!" But when I saw the look in his eyes, it was pretty clear he hadn't meant to hit me. In fact, it was pretty clear he already knew he was doomed. There was no escaping capital punishment for this. As the tears sprang to my eyes, his face only got more and more doomed. I could see the thoughts going through his mind: I killed my sister. What have I done?

I was about eighteen or nineteen when this happened, living at home the summer after my freshman year of college. But even though I was perfectly old enough to take care of myself, I was still happy to sit in the bathroom and let my mom rock me while I cried and held tissues up to my bleeding nose. Over my mom's shoulder, Andrew was hovering a few feet away, also crying, signing "sorry" over and over.

I remember going to work that afternoon, loading trucks for FedEx. My face was a little swollen, but nobody asked me about it. At one point, a box came out of a chute faster than I expected and hit me in the nose. The impact wasn't very hard, but my nose was still tender, even though it wasn't broken. I had to duck into the truck trailer and cry again for a few minutes before I pulled myself together.

35 BACKGROUND NOISE

On one occasion, Dad was giving me a priesthood blessing. I don't remember whether I was sick or seeking spiritual guidance; I just remember sitting on a chair in the dining room while Andrew sat at the table, playing with the salt and pepper shakers. My dad put his hands on my head and began the blessing:

"Rachel—" We heard sounds of clattering, then the sound of the open pepper container hitting the table.

Dad sighed and returned to what he was saying. "I bless you that you will be able—" At this point, we were interrupted by the sound of blowing, as Andrew played with the loose pepper on the table by blowing it around and watching it fly through the air. Dad took his hands off my head to confiscate the open pepper shaker and left Andrew to his blowing. Then he started again where he'd left off.

"Rachel, I bless you—" A sneeze. Another sneeze. "I bless you—" A violent sneeze, followed by a frustrated yell. Another sneeze. Another yell.

"I bless you that—"

Sneeze. "Aaugh!"

"I bless—"

Sneeze. "AAAAAAAUGH!"

Dad was trying to keep going, but his voice was wavering as he tried not to laugh. I could feel his hands shaking. I was just dying trying to hold it in. Both of us just sat there, trying to maintain a sense of reverence as Andrew started pacing around the room angrily, sneezing and shouting with all his might. Every now and then, he got himself together and went back to blow on the pepper again.

We had to give up and clean the pepper off the table. Andrew had to go to his room with some tissues to compose himself.

36 And Now, a Few Words About Vomit

When you add it all up, Andrew has probably spent several years of his life throwing up. When I was in junior high, he spent a few years just kind of spitting up on whatever nearby surface was the hardest to clean. The rug. The dog. The heat vent. The inside of my French horn case.

After about a year of that, his doctor decided he had acid reflux. He prescribed some medication that accomplished nothing. So he upped the dose, and nothing happened. So he upped the dose again, and Andrew started showing negative side effects common to the medication. Still throwing up. When the doctor suggested upping the dose again, Mom decided it was time to switch doctors.

After a good deal of research, we concluded that Andrew was throwing up. That was all we knew. But with a little reward, we found that he could sometimes control it. Dad would take him for a car ride, put a blue Gatorade next to him, and tell him that he could have a "blue drink" and watch trains, if he didn't throw up the whole time. As soon as Andrew threw up, the blue drink went away, and Dad drove home, deliberately avoiding every railroad crossing. This worked like a dream, all up until they came home and Andrew walked through the front door. Bleaugh, all over the carpet. His attitude: whatever, man. I already got to see the trains.

After some fine-tuning, we got a rewards system that was a little longer-lasting, and Andrew started seeing progress. Over time, he forgot to throw up entirely.

After a few years, the vomit came back with a vengeance, and this time, he couldn't control it. He seemed genuinely sorry whenever he threw up, and would go so far as to throw up in a cup, show Mom so he could apologize, then flush the contents down the toilet. After much testing, it was determined that he had celiac—he couldn't eat gluten.

Going gluten-free helped his health somewhat, but he still struggles to hold food down. The current hypothesis is that his damaged heart is just so tired pumping blood that his body doesn't have the get-up-and-go to digest food. The best medication currently: sleep. When he goes to bed earlier, he's less likely to throw up the next day.

He now motivates himself by taking a Sharpie into the bathroom and writing on the back of the toilet tank which foods he's eaten recently. If he held down his food, he draws a smiley face next to it. If he threw it up, it gets a sad face. A few of them have more than one sad face, but the system seems to give him some sense of motivation. And, as an added perk, my parents enjoy explaining the weird-looking grocery list written on the toilet.

On a few occasions, Andrew has thrown up while nobody's home and kept the contents in the nearest container (a bowl or skillet, for example) to show off. If Mom and Dad don't come home in time to validate his remorse, he'll wait on the next-door neighbor's porch, with his bowl, to confess his sins.

37 A WARDROBE MALFUNCTION

I remember one weekend I came home from college for a friend's wedding, honored to be one of the bridesmaids. I was supposed to wear a black Latin skirt and a formal, purple top to the ceremony. I took advantage of the opportunity to wash everything else I owned, while I had easy access to Mom and Dad's washer and dryer.

When I got to the house, I was already running a little late to the wedding, so I dumped my garbage bag full of laundry at the front door, dashed into the bathroom to touch-up my face and hair, and then raced off to the wedding.

Halfway through the reception, I got a call. "Remember your clothes?"

"Yes—wait, what do you mean, *remember*?" I asked.

"Well… we can't find them."

"Okay..."

"...and it's garbage day. And I seem to remember that you had them in a trash bag…"

Oh, no.

"…and it's Andrew's job to take out the garbage on Fridays…"

I laughed. "Well, did you check the can?"

There was an awkward pause. "Well, see, that's the thing. We didn't notice they were missing until after the garbage truck came."

I had ducked into a back room, and I was cracking up. The bride's younger brother had noticed, and was looking at me a little funny. "So what you're telling me," I said loud enough for him to appreciate, "is that all of the clothing I own is now in the city landfill." The bride's brother looked horrified.

"Yes."

"…Except for a Latin skirt and a formal top," I added, looking down at the outfit I was wearing.

"Yes."

I howled. I laughed until tears came to my eyes. "It's okay," I choked out. "I've got thirty bucks. I'll just go to a thrift store tomorrow. Besides," I added, "I needed a change of style."

When I hung up, the bride's brother was frozen in place, staring at me. "Are you okay?" he asked. He looked like he was waiting for a bomb to go off.

I laughed again. "My brother took my laundry out with the trash."

"How much clothing was it?" he asked.

"Pretty much my entire wardrobe. I'd been saving up my laundry so I could do it for free."

He wrung his hands and hung his head. It was like he was mourning my clothing. "Oh, man," he said. "My sister would be a wreck. How are you laughing at this?"

I shrugged. "It's clothes," I said. "And it's not like I spend that much on clothing, anyway. I mean, he's broken nearly everything I own at least once."

It took me nearly ten minutes to reassure him that I wasn't bluffing, about to detonate in tears or rage. I've never cared as much about clothes as most girls do—and I learned at an early age that a good story is worth a little sacrifice. I wasn't panicking; in my head, I was planning the funniest way to tell this story to my roommates.

I did look a little funny the next day, wandering through the thrift store in a bridesmaid's outfit. But I came back to college with a change of style.

38 MISSION ACCEPTED

When I was about halfway through college, I decided to take a break from school and serve as a missionary for my church. Mormon missionaries don't decide their destination—they fill out an application, and church leadership decides where to send them. I was hoping to be sent somewhere exotic, like Taiwan or Zimbabwe. Instead, I was sent to New Jersey.

Andrew was devastated. I hadn't really talked with him a lot about my mission; I wasn't even sure if he knew what a missionary was. I just told him I was going to move out when I got the letter in the mail, and assumed he would think I was back at college.

When I read my mission call out loud, however, he got really emotional. He was sitting next to me on the couch, and by the time I finished the letter, he was crying really hard. He was somewhere between sad and distraught, and he shut himself up in his room for a while. In the meantime, Mom and Dad were so excited they had to look up every satellite map of New Jersey they could possibly find. Dad found all the demographic information of the state for me. Mom found blogs about food.

After their initial excitement (and my initial disappointment) died down, I quietly let myself into Andrew's room. "What's wrong?" I asked. He was sitting on the floor, still crying, rocking back and forth. He just looked up at me and kept crying.

"Are you sad that I'm leaving?" I asked. He kept crying and nodded.

"Well, I'm not leaving for good, you know," I told him. "I'm going on a mission. So I'll be gone for a while, teaching people about Jesus. I want to help people. But I'll come back when I'm done." He looked skeptical.

"I'll be gone a year and a half," I said. "That's a little longer than I was at BYU this last year. And I won't be able to come visit, but I'll send you letters every week, okay?" He nodded. He was starting to pull himself together, and he liked the idea of getting letters every week. I promised to send him letters, and even packages sometimes. He calmed down a bit more.

"Can I still go on a mission?" I asked.

He nodded, crying a little more. But I pinky-promised to write him.

During my mission, I went to Wal-Mart and printed off pictures with the full-year calendar on them. I circled the date I was going to come back, and crossed off all the days that were already over. Andrew loved these. I would usually send one every month or so, assuming he would lose them or wear them out. Andrew liked them so much, he would collect them, cross off the dates, and put them all out on the floor in his room so he could look at them.

After a while, he started asking Mom to cross off the days on her calendar, too. Then he would get impatient and cross off days in advance. Or he would want to take the calendar down, so he could flip through the months and find February 2012, when I was due to come home. He got really mad if the calendar didn't go that far.

After I had been sending these calendars home for a few months, Mom emailed to inform me that she was going paperless and using an online calendar. All the calendars in the house had disappeared. She couldn't find them. She had finally bought a new one, only to have that one disappear. Apparently, only Andrew was allowed to keep calendars.

I kept sending them home.

39 SMOKE, AND ITS CAUSES

One day while I was on my mission, Andrew threw a pair of basketball shorts onto the ceiling fan. The shorts landed up on top, out of reach of the blades, but resting on one of the light bulbs. My parents didn't see it (but probably wondered why the room was suddenly so dark), and Andrew left it there.

After a while, the house began to smell of smoke. Mom was concerned that a fire might have started inside the walls, and hadn't become visible yet. After roaming the house, warning the next-door neighbors, and alerting the fire department, she finally located the source of the smoke in the master bedroom, where the shorts were lying on top of a hot light bulb, smoldering gently.

After Mom removed the shorts and opened a few windows, the house aired out nicely, but the shorts would never be quite the same again. My mom sent them to me in a package, with a handwritten note from Andrew:

> Dear Rachel,
> You will be happy to know I did not burn the house down. I almost did. But I didn't.
> Putting my shorts in the ceiling fan makes the house smell real bad and catches on fire.
> Too bad!
> Thank you for your letter. I am glad they have trains in New Jersey.
> That made me smile.
> I love you!
> Andrew

After reading the letter, I opened the package and found the shorts, with the whole rear region missing and the edges burnt. I held them up for my mission companion to see, and she seemed confused. I'm not sure whether she was more unnerved by the scorched hole, or the odd notion that someone would send me a pair of destroyed shorts in the mail. The shorts hung on the wall above my study desk for several months, an inspiring reminder of home.

40 THE PHONE CALL HOME

Andrew could say a few words when he was in preschool and kindergarten, but he quickly shut up when he realized he could get his point across much more easily with sign. And then, of course, as soon as people started understanding his signs, his signs got sloppy. From an outsider's perspective, Andrew was doing the best he could to communicate. From a sibling's perspective, he was just lazy.

Andrew finally started getting interested in talking just after I left on my mission. I called it a miracle, prompted by my faithful service. My parents said it was because he could finally get a word in edgewise. Regardless of the reason, I was excited and just a little annoyed. I was thrilled he was talking. But of all times he chose to talk, he chose the one time I wasn't there to hear him.

Full-time missionaries are only given two chances every year to call home; the rest of the time, they can email or send hand-written letters. This meant that I couldn't hear Andrew speak until Christmas. We had 45 minutes each to talk with our families, and we would schedule it ahead of time (via email, usually) with our families to make sure everybody was close to the phone.

There was a marked difference between my calls home and my companions' calls home. The dynamic changed, of course, depending on the missionary. Some of my companions came from large families, with siblings, nieces, nephews, grandparents, and sometimes even cousins gathered around the phone at home, all on speaker-phone or taking turns. When someone's family was that large, they would often allot time slots to each family member, allowing 5 or 10 minutes to each family member. My companion would pick up the phone, ask how everybody was doing, and ask how her younger sisters were doing in school, dating, and life generally. She would ask about family members who were engaged, and check up on those who were sick. Those who had smaller families allowed more time for each person, and often had an opportunity to hold a full conversation with each family member.

My phone calls were probably really fun for my companions to listen to, especially hearing only one side of the conversation. I didn't actually have much to say; I could type quickly, so my emails home usually contained all the news from each week. My mom sent emails often enough, there wasn't usually much news from home. So my mom and dad would small-talk with me, tell me how good it was to hear my voice, and tell me a few funny stories. Then they'd ask to talk with my companion for a few minutes and thank her for putting up with me. All of this would happen with the sound of Andrew giggling and yelling in the background.

Then Andrew would take the phone. Here's where it probably got really interesting for my companion. Andrew's sense of humor is kind of like a three-year-old's. When a preschooler first learns to tell jokes, they usually consist of knock-knock jokes with no real punch line, and then hysterical laughter from the preschooler, who thinks he's hilarious. Andrew's usual means of joking is to tell you there's a spider on your head, when there actually isn't.

Every Christmas and Mother's day, I started the conversation something like this: "Hey! Hey, hey! How are you doing? Are you being good? ... What? No! No spiders! There's a spider on your shirt! ... Yes, there is! And it's on fire! ...No, I'm not on fire!" And on and on.

Mom interpreted Andrew's harder sentences, while words like "yes" and "no" were clearly distinguishable. Andrew's vocabulary still wasn't very impressive, but he could say things like, "I love you, Rachel," and "I miss you." Which, of course, moved me to tears.

My companion's view of the conversation was that I talked a lot about spiders and fire, then burst into open weeping and told my brother I loved him. In retrospect, this probably looked pretty weird.

41 COMING HOME

The night I came home from my mission, me and my family went to meet with the Stake President to receive my formal release from missionary service. He told me he understood I had done a good job, and it was time to start a new phase of my life. I cried. I didn't feel ready to start a new phase of my life.

He then ushered me into a room where the Stake High Council was sitting in a meeting, so I could share some of my mission experiences. I had not seen this coming, and I was a little intimidated. Mom, Dad, and Andrew sat in the room with me, waiting for my turn to speak. Andrew was looking at my name tag, which said, "The Church of Jesus Christ of Latter-day Saints" on it. Just below that was my name: "Sister Cope."

Andrew was looking puzzled, trying to figure something out. He signed, "Jesus."

"Yes," I told him. "I've been teaching about Jesus."

He nodded, still looking at my name tag. He touched the place on his own chest where a name tag might go. "Jesus." Then he pantomimed taking the name tag off. "Rachel." He looked back up at me questioningly.

I nodded, tears in my eyes. Mom and Dad looked confused, but I got it. With the name tag, I represented Jesus. Without it, I was just Rachel again. I was crying because I still wanted to be Jesus—but Andrew was excited to have Rachel back. It helped me adjust to home life, remembering that even though I wasn't involved in humanitarian service every day, just being there—and being me—made me important to somebody.

42 MERRY CHRISTMAS TO ALL, AND TO ALL A GOOD FIGHT

About a year before I graduated from college, I went home for the holidays, as I usually did. I felt a little aimless that year, because I was about to graduate and I still didn't really know what I wanted to be when I grew up. I had also just been through a failed relationship, so I wasn't feeling as jolly as most years. Still, I was glad to be home.

My immediate family always reserved Christmas Eve for themselves. We saw extended family on other days, but Christmas Eve was always a close-knit celebration: just Mom, Dad, me, and Andrew. This particular Christmas Eve, we had decided to go to an interdenominational candlelight service just up the street.

Of course, just because the church was a few blocks away didn't mean we were going to walk. Getting Andrew (or my mom, for that matter) to voluntarily walk more than two hundred feet was rare, especially in the snow. So, since it was cold, and since Mom and Andrew were both coming, we drove.

Andrew was upset. This was not the normal routine. It was late (and by "late," I mean "after sunset"), Andrew was tired, and we had never gone to this church before. He was not totally on board with this plan. So when I told him to put his seat belt on, he ignored me. Dad started driving, and I insisted that Andrew put his seat belt on. Andrew was not having it. He yelled in my general direction, and I leaned in to make my point clear.

Unfortunately, that's when Andrew decided to lash out. He punched me in the face.

Once again, my first reaction was to punch him back. Once again, the look on his face convinced me that I didn't need to. He was already horrified. We walked into the church a little awkwardly. The usher greeted

Dad, who was lecturing Andrew. Andrew was distraught, signing "sorry" as emphatically as he could. I came walking straight past the usher, crying a little and sporting a black eye. Merry Christmas. Mom later found me in the bathroom, still crying and trying to clean up my face. There was little blood this time, just a bit of a runny nose and some swelling around my eye. I eventually joined my family, and the Christmas service was really a wonderful, spiritual, and uplifting experience. It just took us a little while to pull ourselves together, that's all.

I still wonder what that usher thought of us.

43 BURNING BABY JESUS

One or two years after the Christmas Eve fistfight, I got a phone call from Mom. Her nativity was ruined. Andrew had thrown the baby Jesus into the fire.

44 THE CASE OF THE VANISHING PANTS

Andrew has an uncanny ability for making things vanish. He also has an uncanny aversion to pants. He hates wearing clothes in general, but pants are a particular nuisance. Andrew went through a phase where he refused to wear pants at all, unless coerced or bribed. Although we successfully got him used to the feeling of "tighty whiteys," the briefs were simply not enough for us (but far too much for him).

There came a day when my brother stumbled upon a genius plan. My mother told him to put on some pants. He ignored her. She persisted. He pretended not to understand. She went to get him some pants—and found they were gone. There were no pants in his dresser. Nor anywhere in the closet. Nor anywhere in his room.

Nor were they to be found in any other closet in the house, the hallway, the laundry basket, the washer, the dryer, the upright piano, the refrigerator, the garage, the chimney, the backyard, the oven, or the garbage disposal. In short, his pants were simply gone.

Mom called me a few hours later from Wal-Mart, where they were replacing Andrew's wardrobe. After buying enough pants to get by, she locked them up in my old room, so he couldn't hide them as quickly. She began a policy of "renting" him one pair at a time, insisting that he had to wear them consistently if he wanted to be able to choose which pants to wear.

Suddenly, pants became a precious and rare commodity. He started wearing them happily, begging for the opportunity to change into a new pair of pants before the first pair became dirty. While Mom was on the phone with me, pleased with the results, she suddenly stopped and said, "Where did you get those?" Her back had been turned for about 2 minutes, during which time he had removed the pants, found an old "vanished" pair, and changed into them. The new pants were now nowhere to be found.

We have no idea where the pants went – and are still going. Old pants still surface from time to time, and new pants still vanish from time to time. We've searched everywhere, but at this point, we've given up. He'll find them when he needs them. We just have to figure out how to convince him that he needs them.

45 Meet the Family

Ethan and I started dating a week before Easter, and we spent that Sunday with my family. Ethan was blown away by the Easter basket my mom made for him. She had bought him candy, a bubble gun, a dinosaur kite, and a stuffed hippopotamus—and packed the lot into a basket with his name on it. At first glance, it would appear my mom thought I was dating a three-year-old. In reality, she would have done this for any grown man.

The second time Ethan saw my family, we were at my parents' house again. Ethan and I were sitting on a couch in the living room, facing my dad on another couch. Dad was monologuing about something or other, and Ethan was trying really hard to listen. I had already heard the story Dad was telling, and I wasn't paying much attention. My eyes wandered around the room and down the hall, where Andrew was strolling casually down the hall away from us, completely naked.

I started laughing quietly, and Ethan turned to see what I was laughing at. His eyes went past my face to the hallway, where my (fully grown) brother was still wandering around nude, and Ethan started laughing with me.

As we sat there, shoulders shaking, Dad just kept talking. After he was done, Ethan apologized, "I'm sorry, Mr. Cope. I didn't mean to laugh at you—it's just that there was a naked man in your hallway."

Dad stood up, completely unconcerned. "Yeah, he does that sometimes," he said, as he started putting his sneakers on. "You should have seen the look on the contractor's face when he saw the little man squatting on the toilet." And then Dad opened the front door and just left. We sat there, confused and laughing, for another twenty minutes. Dad didn't come back.

"He probably went to talk to my neighbor Gary," I said. Later on, we saw Dad and Gary walking across the front yard, carrying a heavy tree limb. He hadn't said a thing to us about yard work.

Later on that day, Ethan saw Andrew come into the hallway (wearing pants this time) and try to go into my old room. He tried the doorknob, found it locked, and sighed, his upper body slumped in defeat. Then he just turned around and found something else to do.

The following year, after we were married, Ethan and I joined my family for Thanksgiving. While the rest of us went next door to watch a movie, Andrew obstinately stayed home, wanting nothing to do with us. We figured he would be fine for a few hours.

When we came back home, we found Andrew in his room, shaving his leg with my dad's electric razor. Mom confiscated the razor while Dad wondered how the dog had gotten so dirty; there was an odd grease-spot in the fur on his back.

Ethan and I were sitting in the guest room talking, when Andrew came into the room. He was laughing. He smiled at us, and we asked what he thought was so funny. "Butter," he signed.

"Butter?" Ethan asked, confused. Down the hallway, we heard bathwater running as Dad tried to get the gunk off the dog's back.

"Dog," Andrew signed. "Butter."

Ethan fought off a laugh and put on his stern face. "Did you butter the dog?"

Huh huh huh, Andrew laughed.

"Do we butter dogs? Is that a nice thing to do?"

Huh huh huh.

"Rachel," Ethan asked, turning to me, "do you think that's funny?"

"Don't ask me that," I said, still fighting back laughter.

Ethan changed his question. "Do you think that's appropriate?"

"No, it's not!"

After some time, we convinced Andrew that buttering family pets was not responsible behavior, and he apologized to the basset hound. Ethan thought it was all hilarious, which is exactly why I married him.

Welcome to my family. This is how we live.

46 An Apology

Things were weird at our house for several reasons—Down syndrome, autism, destructive humor, poor genetic material—but all in all, I don't really feel like my upbringing was that unusual. The specifics were different from most, but I think the basic sibling experience was much the same.

Things sometimes got a little dicey at home, especially while we were teenagers. Although neither of us went out of our way to make life difficult for each other—or our parents—we seemed to have a way of doing it unintentionally.

We were good at irritating one another. There was one day when I came into my bedroom and found Andrew in the process of throwing all my stuff behind the desk. No reason—he just needed something to do, I guess. I snapped, yelled at him, grabbed the stuff out of his hands, and shoved him out of the room.

He was less than pleased. He yelled, banged on the door, and went to his own room. Later, when I thought I should probably apologize, I knocked on his door. When I opened it and he saw who it was, he yelled again, and slammed the door on me. Fine! I stormed off.

We ignored each other for the rest of the day. I had some activity outside the home that evening, so I came back after Andrew was getting ready for bed. He was a little shy around me, but neither of us said anything.

When I got back to my room, I realized that Andrew had been there. He had made my bed. I could tell he had made it himself, because the sheet was still a little bunched in one corner and the blanket was askew— but it was carefully smoothed out on top. He had also put everything back where it belonged, cleaned out from behind the desk, and even emptied the pencil shavings from my mechanical sharpener. For a nonverbal apology, he had outdone himself.

I was humbled. I started to feel a little guilty for being so upset with him in the first place. He was my brother, and no matter what happened, he always would be. Why would I let anything make me forget how much I loved him? Without saying a word, he had let me know that he cared far more about me than whatever we were fighting over.

Silently praying for forgiveness, I promised myself that I would apologize to Andrew first thing in the morning. I turned down the sheets to get into bed.

And that's where I found the pencil shavings.

Epilogue

Andrew Cope is now 23 years old, and lives at home with our parents and a basset hound named Churchill. He has broken 21 toilets and 14 windows. He recently finished his high school diploma through a post-graduation special needs program. He is a ladies' man, and shows off pictures of his many sweethearts. He is a proud, devoted uncle.

He now takes more responsibility to fix the toilets he clogs—he can often be seen walking through the house, with or without pants, wielding a toilet plunger. He takes charge of the laundry and vacuuming, and hopes to get a job soon. He has a piano keyboard in his room, and blasts the pre-loaded demos at teenage volumes and rocks out to them. He is getting more excited about talking, and even occasionally sings.

ABOUT THE AUTHOR

Rachel Unklesbay is a wife, mother, musician, and blogger who enjoys dancing in the kitchen when nobody is looking. She posts new adventures from her own life, as well as current stories about Andrew, on her blog www.sandguppy.wordpress.com.

80707064R00057

Made in the USA
Columbia, SC
20 November 2017